Approaches to Data Design, Engineering, and Development

IDMA 204 COURSE STUDY GUIDE

Insurance Data Management Association (IDMA)
Associate Insurance Data Manager (AIDM)
Designation Program

Technics Publications
SEDONA, ARIZONA

Published by:

115 Linda Vista
Sedona, AZ 86336 USA
www.TechnicsPub.com

Cover design by Lorena Molinari

All rights reserved. No part of this book may be reproduced or transmitted in any form or by any means, electronic or mechanical, including photocopying, recording or by any information storage and retrieval system, without written permission from the publisher, except for the inclusion of brief quotations in a review.

The author and publisher have taken care in the preparation of this book, but make no expressed or implied warranty of any kind and assume no responsibility for errors or omissions. No liability is assumed for incidental or consequential damages in connection with or arising out of the use of the information or programs contained herein.

All trade and product names are trademarks, registered trademarks or service marks of their respective companies and are the property of their respective holders and should be treated as such.

Unless otherwise apparent, examples used in this course are based on hypothetical situations and are for educational purposes only. The characters, persons, products, services, and organizations described in these examples are fictional. Any similarity or resemblance to any other character, person, product, services, or organization is merely coincidental. IDMA is not responsible for such coincidental or accidental resemblances.

This material may contain website links external to IDMA. IDMA neither approves nor endorses any information, products, or services to which any external websites refer. Nor does IDMA control these websites' content or the procedures for website content development.

IDMA materials related to this course are provided with the understanding that IDMA is not engaged in rendering legal, accounting, or other professional service. Nor is IDMA explicitly or implicitly stating that any of the processes, procedures, or policies described in the materials are the only appropriate ones to use. The advice and strategies contained herein may not be suitable for every situation.

Without in any way limiting the author's exclusive rights under copyright, any use of this publication to "train" generative artificial intelligence (AI) technologies to generate text is expressly prohibited. The author reserves all rights to license uses of this work for generative AI training and the development of machine learning language models.

First Edition

First Printing 2026

Copyright © 2026 Insurance Data Management Association, Inc. (IDMA)

ISBN, print ed.   9798898161149
ISBN, Kindle ed.   9798898161156
ISBN, PDF ed.   9798898161163

Library of Congress Control Number: 2026942077

Contents

Introduction

Founded in 1983, IDMA is an independent nonprofit professional association dedicated to increasing the level of professionalism, knowledge, and visibility of insurance data management through education, research, annual forums, local chapter meetings, news bulletins, and peer-to-peer networking. It serves individuals employed in any aspect of insurance data management. This includes individuals engaged in any of the following enterprise information governance activities within various functional areas of insurance companies, regulatory bodies, statistical/rating organizations, industry consulting firms, professional associations and learned societies, and technology research and services providers:

- data definition
- data collection
- data administration
- data standards
- data processing
- data analysis
- internal and external data reporting
- data quality.

The main objective of IDMA is the administration of an educational program designed to increase professional proficiency and to provide a professional designation in the data management discipline. Additionally, IDMA provides an ongoing forum for the discussion of issues and innovations in data management through technical seminars, educational workshops, and publications.

IDMA courses, workshops, and forums are highly recommended for a broad audience including new hires, IT and data modeling professionals who want to broaden their knowledge of the business side of insurance data management, anyone who manages and governs data in the industry (statistical, or management information data), and anyone who needs to use or communicate good quality data/information – from actuaries to underwriters, and claims and analytics professionals.

Students who complete the four IDMA-developed courses and successfully pass the examinations are awarded an *Associate Insurance Data Manager (AIDM®)* designation. The IDMA courses may be taken in any order; there are no prerequisites. However, the courses are numbered to indicate a recommended sequence.

Students who complete additional course work from other selected insurance industry educational organizations and successfully pass the specified examinations receive the *Certified Insurance Data Manager (CIDM®)* designation.

For details on the designation requirements, please refer to the IDMA website at www.IDMA.org or call our office at +1 (201) 469-3069.

Using this Course Guide

This course guide will help you learn the course content and prepare for the exam.

Almost all assignments in this course guide, except for the final assignment, which is a recap of the prior assignments, include the following components:

- **Educational Objectives.** These are the most important study tools in the course guide. Because all of the questions on the exam are based on the Educational Objectives, the best way to study for the exam is to focus on these objectives.

- **Key Terms and Concepts.** These terms and concepts are fundamental to understanding the assignment. After completing the required reading, test your understanding of the assignment's Key Terms and Concepts by writing their definitions.

- **Review Questions.** The review questions test your understanding of what you have read. Review the Educational Objectives and required reading, then answer the questions to the best of your ability. When you are finished, check the answers at the end of the assignment to evaluate your comprehension.

- **Discussion Questions.** These questions are intended to continue to test your knowledge of the required reading by applying what you've studied to real-life situations. No suggested answers are provided at the end of the assignment for these types of open discussion questions. Answers may vary by student and will depend on their organization's culture, resources, and processes.

Important Note Applicable to All IDMA Course Material: IDMA strives to keep all of its course material current. The information provided is up to date at the time of publication. The timing and pace of industry changes, along with the constraints of publication, can at times result in a lag in updates being included. IDMA regularly reviews content to ensure that it is current and will publish updates as necessary and appropriate.

Exam Information

IDMA exams are given online, consist of 100 multiple-choice and true/false type questions, and are three hours long. Unofficial scores are tabulated and issued immediately after the exam completion. Official scores are mailed to students within 15 business days after the conclusion of the exam cycle. The passing score is 70%.

Students are allowed to take more than one course exam during an exam cycle. Students are also allowed to retake an exam within the same exam cycle if they were not successful on their first try.

Exams are conducted with no reference materials, papers, books, or other aids permitted in the room. No student may communicate with another during the exam. Students are not allowed to maintain copies of their exams. All exam materials are considered the property of IDMA.

Exam Registration Information and Requirements

Currently, IDMA does not contract with testing centers (such as Prometric, Pearson, and Kryterion) to host its exams onsite. IDMA exams are given, so far as possible, at the student's worksite with the cooperation of the human resources or education department in locating a proctor and site.

NOTE: Students are responsible for locating a proctor and providing IDMA with the proctor's contact information. A proctor could be anyone from your HR department, your manager, or a staffer. A week before the exam, IDMA will email your proctor a "proctor package" that explains the exam process. You will also receive your exam pass via email around the same time.

The purchase of the study guide for the current IDMA course does not automatically register a candidate for the examination. As you proceed with your studies, be sure to arrange for your exam.

- Visit our website at www.IDMA.org to access and print the exam registration form, which contains information and forms needed to register for your exam.
- Plan to register with IDMA well in advance of your exam. Late fees apply two weeks prior to the start of the exam cycle.
- Coordinate with your proctor on the exam date and start time.

How to Study for IDMA Exams

Use the assigned study materials (textbook and course guide). Focus your study on the Educational Objectives presented at the beginning of each course guide assignment. Thoroughly read the textbook and any other assigned materials, and then complete the course guide exercises. Choose a study method that best suits your needs; for example, participate in a traditional class, an informal study group, or study on your own. IDMA recommends that you begin your studies for the exam at least two months before your scheduled exam date.

Student Resources

For more information on any of the IDMA publications, course examinations, and other services:

- Visit our website at www.IDMA.org.
- Call us at +1 (201) 469-3069.

- Fax us at +1 (201) 748-1690.
- Write to us at Insurance Data Management Association (IDMA), 545 Washington Boulevard, 16th Floor, Jersey City, NJ 07310.

Data Quality Management for Insurance

Educational Objectives

Upon completion of this assignment, you should be able to:

1. Describe the idea of data as an organizational asset, as well as the characteristics of data that differentiate it from other assets.
2. Explain the connection of data to the insurance life cycle, both in general and in relation to specific functions within the life cycle.
3. Describe the general costs of poor-quality data, the specific risks and costs of poor-quality data within the insurance industry, and the opportunities associated with high-quality data within various insurance functions.
4. Introduce the concept of data quality management.
5. Describe responsibilities for data quality within an insurance organization.

For each assignment, define or describe each of the Key Terms and Concepts and answer each of the Review and Discussion Questions.

Key Terms and Concepts

Asset:

Meta Asset:

Resources:

Underwriting:

Combined Ratio:

Data Quality Management:

Fit-For-Purpose Data:

Data Consumers:

Review Questions

1. Identify the categories of assets and provide examples of each.

2. Data fits best in which of the asset categories?

   A. Financial.
   B. Physical.
   C. Human.
   D. Intangible.

3. How does data differ from other assets?

4. True or False: The differences between data and other types of assets make it easier to manage data.

5. How does data support the transfer of risk in an insurance transaction?

6. What does a combined ratio greater than 1.00 indicate and how does data enter into the considerations?

7. Identify the phases of the insurance product lifecycle.

8. What role does data play in the insurance product life cycle?

9. What data is important to the product development phase of the insurance product lifecycle?

10. What data is important to the business development phase of the insurance product lifecycle?

11. Data from the distribution channel management phase of the insurance product lifecycle feeds which other phases?

12. Better data during the distribution channel management phase of the insurance product lifecycle helps:

13. What data is important to the underwriting phase of the insurance product lifecycle?

14. What data is important to the claim administration phase of the insurance product lifecycle?

15. True or False: Better data during the claim administration phase of the insurance product lifecycle helps detect fraud and reduce costs related to fraud.

16. How does the compliance/legal/regulatory requirements phase interact with other phases of the insurance product lifecycle with respect to data?

17. Better data during the compliance/legal/regulatory requirements phase of the insurance product lifecycle helps:

18. How can data requirements affect the quality of data?

19. How can people affect the quality of data?

20. What changing conditions might affect data needed by the insurance industry?

21. True or False: Changing conditions can reduce the value of data as well as the cost to create and use data.

22. Identify the direct costs of using poor data.

23. Describe the indirect or hidden costs of poor-quality data.

24. Poor-quality data impacts insurance company operations and performance by:

25. True or False: The quality of the insurance company's data doesn't affect the insurer's ability to create opportunity and improve performance.

26. Fit for purpose has measurable characteristics such as:

27. What does it mean for fit-for-purpose data to be usable?

28. True or False: The purpose of data quality management is to store data in a secure ensvironment.

29. Identify and describe the data management practices used to build trust in data.

30. Why is building trust so important in the insurance industry?

31. True or False: Ensuring data quality is the responsibility of the IT department.

32. What is the role of data governance professionals in ensuring data quality?

33. What is the role of data stewards in ensuring data quality?

Discussion Questions

NOTE: The questions below are intended to continue to challenge you to test your knowledge of the required reading by applying what you have studied to real-life situations.

No suggested answers are provided at the end of the assignment for these types of open discussion questions. Answers may vary by student and will depend on their organization's culture, resources, and processes.

1. Describe how the data management role is distributed in your organization.

2. Does your organization have an enterprise perspective on data management? If so, describe how it has influenced data quality? If not, how would such a perspective be implemented, and what value would it bring?

Answers to Assignment 1 Questions

NOTE: These answers are provided to give students a basic understanding of acceptable types of responses. They are often not the only valid answers and are not intended to provide an exhaustive response to the questions.

Key Terms and Concepts

Asset: A resource controlled by the enterprise as a result of past events and from which future economic benefits are expected to flow to the enterprise. (Per the International Financial Reporting Standards (IFRS) framework).

Meta Asset: Describes other assets.

Resources: Things available for use.

Underwriting: The process of assessing risk based on rating factors, which will differ depending on the purpose of the insurance.

Combined Ratio: Ratio of losses and expenses associated with claims to premium.

Data Quality Management: The application of quality management practices to data.

Fit-For-Purpose Data: Data that has fundamental, measurable characteristics that reflect commonsense assumptions about quality.

Data Consumers: The processes, systems, and people who use data.

Review Questions

1. Categories of assets are:
    *   **Financial:** Cash or cash equivalents, accounts receivable, investments, and other instruments that have direct, measurable economic value, even if this value fluctuates under different conditions.
    *   **Physical:** Buildings, furniture, vehicles, and other physical assets that are required for the organization to function, and which the organization must purchase and maintain. Like financial assets, physical assets have clearly measurable economic value.
    *   **Human:** Employees, contractors, partners, and management – the people who are trained and paid to work for the organization and who use their skills, knowledge, and experience to meet organizational objectives.
    *   **Intangible:** Intellectual property, patents, brand recognition, goodwill – factors that all organizations have, and which can differentiate them from their competitors, but for which it is more challenging to assign specific economic value.

2. D Intangible.

3. Data differs from other assets in the following ways:
   - Data is not "consumed" when it is used. The same data can be used multiple times for different purposes and not be used up.
   - Data can be shared among multiple users, even at the same time.
   - While data is easy to copy and share, it is not easy to re-create, because data is unique to the organization, process, and context in which it is produced.
   - Data's value changes over time and across contexts. Usability, uses, and interpretation of the meaning of data will differ between data consumers.
   - Data changes shape. It is often manipulated, combined, aggregated, or otherwise transformed when used.
   - The use of data often creates more data.
   - Because data about the same objects, entities, and events can be captured at different points in time, data provides a perspective on change itself.

4. False. It is more challenging to manage data than other assets, especially to manage data quality.

5. Knowledge gained from data collected from past events allows risks to be pooled. This data allows for the calculation of probabilities around the risk for individual members of a defined population (more data). This knowledge allows a premium to be determined.

6. First, loss, expense, and premium are data, as is the combined ratio. If the combined ratio exceeds one, the insurer must evaluate aspects of its process (from the type of product it sells, the markets it sells in, the population it sells to, its distribution network, its underwriting, pricing, reserving, and claim administration practices, and how it serves its policyholders) to ascertain what changes to make to improve its performance. This type of evaluation is completely dependent on having the right data and having confidence that the data is reliable (complete, accurate, timely).

7. The phases of the insurance product lifecycle are:
   - Product Development identifies insurable risks, determines how to price them, and creates or modifies products to transfer risk.
   - Business Development identifies markets, potential customers, and strategies for selling products to new customers and for retaining existing customers. Includes new business, renewals, and cross-selling.
   - Distribution Channel Management, where applicable, partners with agents, brokers, and other distributors, establishes technologies through which to sell insurance products and compensate partners (managing contracts, commissions, agency relationships, etc.).
   - Underwriting assesses and prices the risk of specific potential purchasers, reserves appropriately based on risk factors and past experience.
   - Customer Service/Policy Administration issues and maintains policy (cancellations, reinstatements, renewals, payments, maturities, beneficiaries); responds to customer inquiries (call center activities, customer self-service).
   - Claim Administration pays claims fairly, accurately, and on time; handles other claim functions, including adjudication, processing, payment analysis (over/underpayment, fraud, recovery), and billing (processing, collection, subrogation).
   - Compliance/Regulatory/Legal demonstrates that business has been conducted in conformance with the law, government regulation, industry requirements, and ethical business practices.

8. Data is critical to each phase in the insurance product life cycle, and each phase produces output used in subsequent phases. Indeed, data binds the different phases together. Data from any and all phases can be used to generate insight about individual phases and the overall process.

9. To identify and analyze insurable risks, data about those risks are needed: how often they are likely to happen, where they are likely to happen, conditions that might contribute to their happening, and the costs associated with them.

10. Developing business opportunities requires information about the people and organizations who are or might be motivated to insure against specific risks: where they live and work; how and why they are impacted by the risks; what motivates them to purchase insurance.

11. Agents and brokers can bring insights into the marketplace for business and product development. Agents and brokers can provide information on policyholders to underwriting and claims administration.

12. Better data during the distribution channel management phase of the insurance product lifecycle helps:
    - Identify, engage, and retain effective partners.
    - Improve relationships with agents and brokers.
    - Optimize the distribution chain.
    - Model factors that improve lead generation and placement rates.
    - Identify new distribution channels.

13. Once a potential customer is identified, underwriting the account requires additional data about that customer and the risk factors that will impact their premium. Risk factors themselves are understood through the past claims experience of other policyholders.

14. To pay claims accurately and on time requires information about the claim event itself, the customer impacted by the event, details of the policy that insures against the event, and the organizations responding to the event (for example, in the case of a car accident, the car repair shop).

15. True.

16. All phases of the insurance lifecycle must collect and manage data required to demonstrate compliance with laws, regulations, and insurance industry standards.

17. Better data during the compliance/legal/regulatory requirements phase of the insurance product lifecycle helps:
    - Respond in a timely and accurate way to compliance requirements.
    - Improve the efficiency of regulatory reporting, reduce the time required for research, and reduce the need for rework.

18. Data requirements may be:
    - Unknown or undefined.
    - Ambiguously defined.
    - Defined inconsistently within an organization or across life cycle phases.

19. People who collect data may:
    - Make errors.
    - Misunderstand data requirements.
    - Interpret requirements in different ways.
    - Lack of understanding of why requirements are important.
    - Lack of training on how to record data.
    - Lack the information they need to verify data.
    - Act with malicious intent and deliberately misrepresent "facts".

People who use data may:
- Not be able to find the data they need.
- Use data that is incomplete, incorrect, or out of date.
- May use data for analyses for which it was not intended.
- Require data that does not exist/has not been collected, or is not in a form they can use.
- Misunderstand data (think it represents something it does not represent).
- Interpret data incorrectly (get incorrect "insight" from the data).

20. Data is evolving, as is the need for data to support and influence business opportunities, partnerships (e.g., agents and brokers), customer needs, and risk factors. Laws and regulations change or new ones are added. Ideas change (e.g., the concept of gender).

21. False. The value of data may be reduced, but the cost to create and use it may be increased.

22. The direct costs of using poor data include:
- Costs in preparing reconciliations.
- Failure to bill or collect receivables.
- Lost sales.
- Inability to deliver orders.
- Inability to respond to customer inquiries.
- Failure to meet contractual requirements or service level agreements.
- Delays in implementing new systems.
- Scrap and rework required to detect and remediate issues.

23. The indirect or hidden costs of poor-quality data include:
- **Inefficiencies**: Process failures and delays, impact to project timelines, reduced productivity due to activities such as time spent looking for and cleansing data, correcting data (often multiple times), and creating workarounds.
- **Customer Impact**: Customer dissatisfaction, increased customer service costs, and customer attrition.
- **Organizational Impact**: Mistrust, interpersonal conflict, and employee dissatisfaction.
- **Impediments to Improvement**: Failure in reengineering or reorganization efforts; inability to innovate.
- **Inability to execute business strategy**: Bad decision-making, missed opportunities, limits on execution, failure to gain a competitive advantage.
- **Reputational costs**: Direct costs of non-compliance (e.g., fines) and public relations/damage control; indirect costs of poor reputation.

24. Poor-quality data impacts insurance company operations and performance by:
- Causing inefficient execution of operational work, which affects the bottom line.
- Reducing the company's ability to meet legal, regulatory, and compliance requirements.
- Reducing the company's ability to identify actionable insights through analytics.
- Increasing the chance that any insights will be misleading.

25. False. High-quality data can create opportunities and improve an organization's ability to act on them.

26. Fit for purpose has measurable characteristics such as:
- **Accurate/Correct**: The information correctly represents what it purports to represent. It does not contain errors.

- **Complete**: All the records required for the purpose are available. These records are fully populated with all required (mandatory) information. They may also contain supplementary (e.g., optional) information.
- **Current/Timely**: The information is up-to-date for the purpose. Attributes that change over time have the most recent information.
- **Accessible**: Data must be available for use in decisions and other actions.
- **Consistent with business rules**: If data values are not consistent with business rules, then either the data is incorrect or the rules themselves have been broken.
- **Relevant**: The data must be able to answer the questions that people are asking of it.

27. Usable means the data is accessible and exists in a format that enables a data customer (a person, process, or system) to take action with the data.

28. False. The purpose of data management is to build trust in data, which may include storing it in a secure environment, but also entails much more.

29. The data management practices used to build trust in data include:
    - **Data Standards**: Formally defining expectations for data through data standards.
    - **Data Assessment**: Assessing data in applications and data repositories against standards.
    - **Data Quality Reporting**: Reporting on the quality of data in applications and repositories.
    - **Data Issue Management**: Managing data quality issues from discovery through remediation.
    - **Business and Technical Process Improvement**: Identifying the root causes of data issues and implementing process controls and other improvements to prevent errors.

30. Insurance itself is built on the idea of trust and is dependent on data to do its work and make good on its promises. Data not only binds the organization and the life cycle phases together, it also represents the work of the organization and the organization's relationships with its customers and partners, including regulators and other stakeholders.

31. False. Everyone who creates or uses data in the organization has a role to play to ensure data quality.

32. Data governance professionals should oversee the management of the organization's data by facilitating the development of policies and standards that enable the creation of complete, correct, consistent, and usable data. Data governance professionals should also educate the organization.

33. Data stewards should help others in the organization create value from data by sharing their expertise on the data itself and on the governance processes that serve as guardrails to enable use and prevent misuse of data.

Understanding Data

Educational Objectives

Upon completion of this assignment, you should be able to:

1. Define data in depth in order to understand the risks associated with data creation/production and use, and to recognize differences in the perspectives of data producers and consumers.
2. Describe why understanding how data is produced and used is critical to data quality management (quality management history will come later, but the customer is the arbiter of quality).
3. Explain what it means for data to be a "product" instead of a "by-product" of organizational processes.
4. Explain what metadata is and why documented knowledge about data is critical to data use.
5. Explain the concept of data literacy and some of the fundamental knowledge, skills, and experience required to understand and interpret data.
6. Explain factors within an organization that can affect the quality of data (culture's relation to quality, data literacy/awareness of the role data plays in insurance, knowledge of, and level of maturity of data management practices).

For each assignment, define or describe each of the Key Terms and Concepts and answer each of the Review and Discussion Questions.

Key Terms and Concepts

Entities:

Attributes:

Data

Product:

By-Product:

Data Consumers:

Metadata:

Data Literacy:

Knowledge of Data-as-Data:

Review Questions

1. True or False: Most organizations create data intentionally so that it is carefully designed for use beyond its initial creation.

2. True or False: Data that has been intentionally created for a specific purpose and meets the requirements of that purpose will likely not meet the requirements for other purposes.

3. High-quality data:

4. In the realm of science and statistics, describe the use and design of data.

5. Even for scientific and statistical purposes, there are limits to data quality, such as:

6. Identify some aspects of data creation.

7. How does commerce data differ from science and statistical data? Why is this important?

8. Why do differences exist between how scientific and business data are collected?

9. What challenges are companies finding as they attempt to leverage data science to improve their understanding of customers, products, and distribution channels?

10. Why do business processes make it difficult to leverage data to improve understanding of customers, products, and distribution channels?

11. True or False: Data definitions are enough to ensure that data from different departments using different technologies are easy to integrate.

12. Different data consumers will likely have different requirements based on their intended uses. What assumptions can be made as a good starting point for data quality improvement?

13. Why is the relationship between data use and actual data produced not simple in the insurance industry?

14. How do people affect data collection and data quality?

15. How does technology affect data quality?

16. Identify some ways in which technologies from different processes can affect data quality.

17. True or False: For organizations to produce high-quality data and to get value from that data requires focus and cultural orientation toward quality.

18. Identify and describe the important factors that need to come together to produce and use high-quality data in the insurance industry.

19. True or False: Effective interpretation of data to draw accurate conclusions requires either metadata or data literacy, but not necessarily both.

20. True or False: Metadata is always of high quality and therefore does not present any data quality issues.

21. How does the data literacy level of users influence the perception of data quality?

22. Identify some of the aspects of metadata.

23. Identify the kinds of information that might be included in the metadata about a data object.

24. Identify the kinds of information that might be included in the metadata about a data field.

25. Identify types of information for which an organization may consider collecting metadata.

26. Identify forms of documentation for which an organization may consider collecting metadata.

27. True or False: Knowledgeable insurance subject matter experts (SME) rarely need to reference metadata.

28. How is general literacy the foundation of data literacy?

29. What does it mean that data literacy is multi-tiered?

30. Data Literacy is on a continuum. What does that mean?

31. How is data literacy determined by the individual's role in the organization?

32. What concepts are included in knowledge of data-as-data?

33. Knowledge of data within an industry is a form of domain knowledge. The insurance industry requires an understanding of what types of information?

34. What thinking skills are needed to process and use data?

35. Identify some common skills needed for data sense-making.

36. Not everyone uses data on a daily basis. What are some opportunities that can be implemented to use and manipulate data in day-to-day activities?

Discussion Questions

NOTE: The questions below are intended to continue to challenge you to test your knowledge of the required reading by applying what you have studied to real-life situations.

No suggested answers are provided at the end of the assignment for these types of open discussion questions. Answers may vary by student and will depend on their organization's culture, resources, and processes.

1. Discuss the kinds of metadata you use.

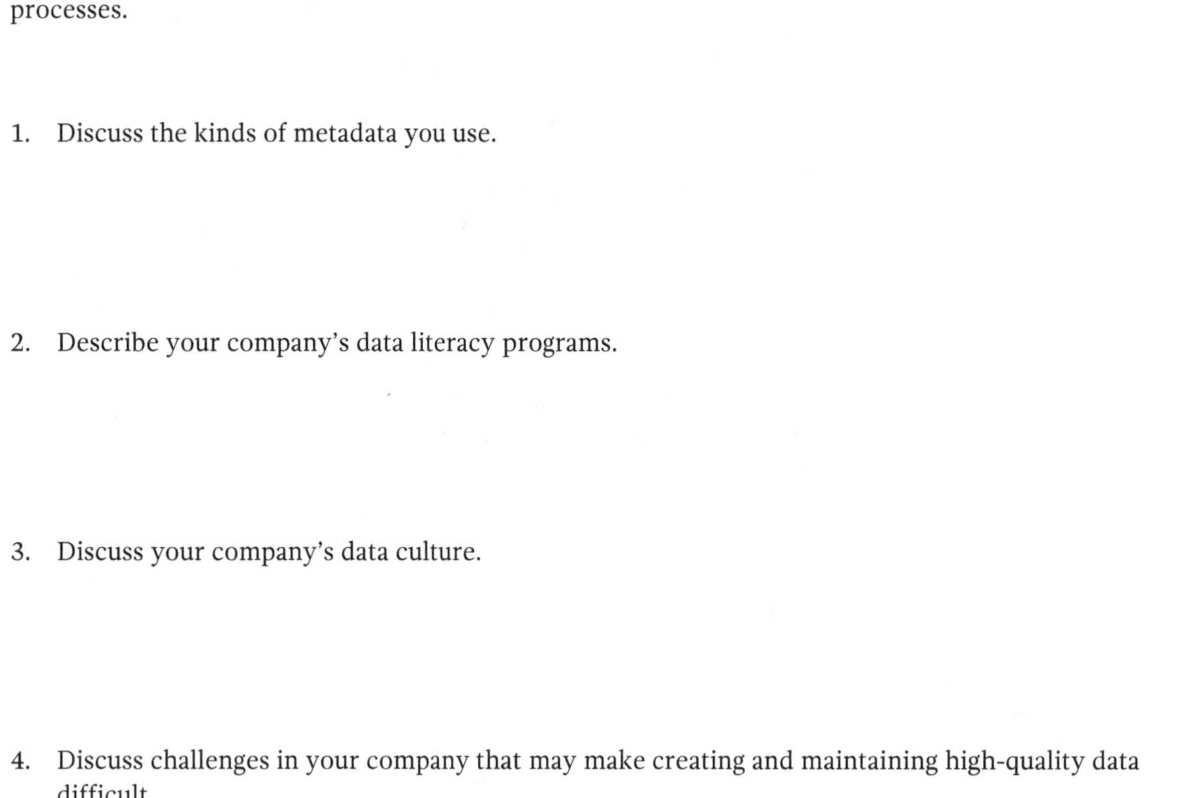

2. Describe your company's data literacy programs.

3. Discuss your company's data culture.

4. Discuss challenges in your company that may make creating and maintaining high-quality data difficult.

Answers to Assignment 2 Questions

NOTE: These answers are provided to give students a basic understanding of acceptable types of responses. They are often not the only valid answers and are not intended to provide an exhaustive response to the questions.

Key Terms and Concepts

Entities: Things about which an organization requires knowledge.

Attributes: Characteristics of entities.

Data: The representation of selected characteristics of objects, events, and concepts, expressed and understood through explicitly defined conventions related to their meaning, collection, and storage. This is the scientific and statistical definition.

Product: Output made with the intention of meeting customer requirements.

By-Product: An accidental output from a process that is assumed to have little value and is often ignored.

Data Consumers: The people, processes, and systems that use data. Data consumers are the final arbiters of quality.

Metadata: Documented knowledge about data. Refers to the context of data needed to understand the data, which is a form of data itself that must exist in an explicit form.

Data Literacy: Refers to the ability to read, understand, interpret, and learn from data in different contexts, and to apply what is learned in one context to new contexts. It encompasses the skills, knowledge, and experience required to understand and use data, and to communicate with other people about data.

Knowledge of Data-as-Data: Refers to understanding the processes and technologies through which data is created, used, and understood.

Review Questions

1. False. Most organizations create data as a by-product of organizational activities; therefore, the data are not well designed.

2. True.

3. High-quality data:
    *   Provides an accurate, clear, comprehensible representation of reality.
    *   May be fit for some purposes but not others based on the way the data is organized, the level of grain, and the level of detail.
    *   Can not be expected to exist in exactly the shape users want and need.

4. For science and statistics, data is collected for a purpose – to answer the questions the scientist or statistician wants to answer or to test a hypothesis. Data is designed in the sense that choices about what data to collect are driven by the goals of the study and are generally collected with care, often under controlled conditions.

5. Data and its use benefit from a degree of skepticism. We expect data to represent facts. The choices made about what data to collect influence how we perceive the world. Moreover, the choices of what entities and attributes to collect may miss important characteristics of the data.

6. Some aspects of data creation include:
   - There are different ways of representing objects, concepts, and events.
   - The choices people make about what characteristics to represent and how to represent them are driven by the purposes for representing the objects, concepts, and events in the first place.
   - These choices will influence the structure and the level of detail in the data that is collected.
   - These choices may be motivated by drivers other than the immediate goals of the data collection.
   - They are also influenced by the perceptions, beliefs, and biases of those determining what data to collect and how to represent that data. This influence may be conscious or unconscious.

7. In a business setting, most commerce data is not designed and collected with scientific rigor or statistical discipline. It is collected to meet the requirements of business processes so that business can be transacted, often through applications and processes that are designed independently of one another. This means that while some data may be recognizably "the same" across processes and applications (and therefore within the insurance product life cycle), data may be structured differently, records may represent entities at different levels of grain, attributes may have different names and different levels of precision, sets of valid values may differ from each other, and so on.

8. Scientific data are designed and collected with rigor and discipline to meet a specific purpose. Business data are the result of historical conditions and the evolution of the business processes and technology.

9. Much of the work of data scientists involves cleaning, reconciling, and preparing data for use in algorithms and models. Even data that is correct in its original setting may be inconsistent across other datasets. From a data consumer perspective, this is a data quality issue.

10. Business processes that create data were originally set up to complete business transactions. As a result, they are not viewed as a data production process. The created data is a by-product of these processes and an accidental output that may be assumed to have little value or often ignored.

11. False. Defined and followed data standards are necessary for integration.

12. While different consumers may have different intended uses for the same data, they are more likely to have many common requirements than to have substantially different requirements. This commonality is a good starting point for data improvement.

13. The breadth of data consumers and data uses is wide. Data produced in one part of the organization is not only used by other processes in the insurance product lifecycle, but also by reporting and analytic functions, including business intelligence and data science. The data must meet the requirements of regulators and data collection organizations/statistical agents.

14. People affect data collection and data quality in the following ways:
   - People make choices about what data to create based on the purpose for which the data is collected.
   - The choices of data depend on the skills and experience of the people making the choice.

- People make choices about which characteristics to collect and how to represent those characteristics.
- They use different units of measurement, different languages, and different lists of valid values.
- They organize tables so that rows represent entities with different levels of granularity.
- People use unstructured data, which must be given structure or mined for meaning.
- People choose how to analyze the data driven by the questions they want to answer.
- People choose the technology used to store and analyze data.

15. Data is stored using different technologies, resulting in different, inconsistent structures and formats. Tools to access and aggregate data may be different or work differently.

16. Some ways in which technologies from different processes affect data quality are:
- Data may be defined differently, either structurally (different definitions of an entity or attribute) or in terms of the precision of the values.
- The meaning of the data and use of the fields may change over time.
- Technical constraints can limit how much data can be collected and in what format, for example, byte limits on social media and field length on mainframe systems.
- The absence of controls, edits, and validations that enforce quality rules allows invalid data to be entered into an application.
- Different systems may handle numbers differently, such as the number of decimal points or the rules for rounding.
- Differences in how data are organized and stored, for example, the redundancy in flat files or how to store numbers (with or without leading zeros), and how to store text fields like SSNs.

17. True.

18. The important factors that need to come together to produce and use high-quality data in the insurance industry are:
- **Awareness**: People within the organization must understand the role data plays in binding the insurance processes together; how the overall data represents the organization's activities, creating a holistic picture of how the organization works. Awareness means understanding that the binding of processes together brings value.
- **Leadership and Cultural Commitment**: Insurance company data is complex. The organization must commit to making the data better, which requires leadership.
- **Oversight and Governance**: A data governance program formalizes desired behaviors through policy, supports consistency through data standards, and enables data use through metadata management and data stewardship.
- **Accountability**: People within the organization must understand their role in data production and use. Producers must know who uses the data and ensure that it meets the requirements of the data consumers. Consumers must get their requirements in front of producers so they can be met.
- **Metadata Management**: The encoded data needs to be decoded and interpreted, so management of the formal data is key to success.
- **Ongoing Education and Data Literacy Development**: Producing high-quality data requires training. As conditions change, data producers and consumers need to be made aware of the changes and have the ability to evolve their roles. This requires ongoing education to improve their data literacy.

19. False. Both metadata and data literacy are needed to effectively draw conclusions from data.

20. False. Metadata itself must be of high quality. Otherwise, it presents data quality issues.

21. Users who are more literate ask different questions and observe different data characteristics than those with less developed data interpretation skills.

22. Aspects of metadata include:
    - Defines data and describes relationships.
    - Provides knowledge of the processes that create data.
    - Provides an understanding of the ways data is organized and used.

23. The kinds of information that might be included in the metadata about a data object include:
    - System/database the object exists in.
    - Plain Language Name.
    - Physical/Query-able Name.
    - Purpose.
    - Business processes that produce the data in the object.
    - Source system(s) that populate the object.
    - Update frequency of the object.
    - Update Type: full refresh, incremental update, incremental with change data capture.
    - Data Domain/Subject Area.
    - Relationships to other objects.
    - Security Classification of the object.
    - Privacy Level of data in the object.
    - Restrictions on Use.
    - Regulatory Impact. That is, is the data in the object subject to regulatory requirements?
    - Business Owner.
    - Technical Owner.

24. The kinds of information that might be included in the metadata about a data field include:
    - Object the field is part of.
    - Plain Language Name.
    - Physical/Query-able Name.
    - Definition.
    - Data Type and/or format.
    - Privacy information. That is, is the field considered personally identifiable information?
    - Domain of Valid Values.
    - Rules for Population.
    - Data Quality Rules.

25. Types of information for which an organization may consider collecting metadata include:
    - Business Processes.
    - Systems/Applications.
    - Data Lineage and the Data Supply Chain.
    - The Logic embedded in Data Processing Routines.
    - The Results of Data Processing Routines.
    - Business Intelligence Reports.
    - Analytic Models.

26. Forms of documentation for which an organization may consider collecting metadata include:
    - Architectural patterns.
    - Architectural diagrams.

- Data Models: conceptual, logical, and physical.
- Data Flow diagrams.
- Data Requirements.
- Technical Specifications.
- Data Quality Standards and Rules.
- System/application requirements.
- Source to target mapping documents.
- Log files.

27. False. Insurance companies have so much data for an individual to understand everything about all of it.

28. General literacy is the ability to read, write, and understand written texts. Data itself is a kind of written text. The skills necessary to mirror general literacy skills include the ability to translate and interpret abstract symbols, to hold multiple time frames in mind, and to understand the progression of ideas.

29. Data literacy requires general knowledge of data-as-data, knowledge of data used within the industry and specific knowledge of the data used within the organization.

30. Data Literacy is on a continuum in that a person is not data literate or data illiterate. Individuals have some level of literacy. They develop and hone their skills by learning about data (knowledge) and applying what they learn (experience).

31. The level of data literacy required of any individual within an organization depends on their role and their data-related responsibilities. Data scientists require deep knowledge of statistics. Business Intelligence developers require deep knowledge of data visualization techniques. Data quality analysts require the ability to work with both statistical patterns and basic visualizations.

32. The following concepts are included in the knowledge of data-as-data:
    - The data life cycle.
    - Processes for data collection and/or creation.
    - Organizing data, choices in data structure.
    - Data risk, things that can go wrong when data is collected/created; how errors can be prevented.
    - Data maintenance processes.
    - Data protection and security.
    - Data transformation, including standardization, aggregation, and visualization.
    - Data integration.
    - Data uses.

33. The insurance industry requires an understanding of the following types of information:
    - Types of data required to understand products, customers, vendors, and transactions.
    - Data required for customer service.
    - Data required for business intelligence.
    - Data required for regulatory reporting.

34. Thinking skills needed to process and use data include:
    - The ability to understand what data represents.
    - To see the patterns in it.
    - To interpret and draw conclusions from it.

35. Common skills needed for data sense-making include:
    - **Critical thinking**: Recognizing how you think, avoiding logical fallacies, remaining open minded, seeing a problem from multiple perspectives before drawing a conclusion.
    - **Scientific thinking**: Applying a scientific approach to problems; asking effective questions; formulating approaches to testing hypotheses.
    - **Quantitative reasoning**: Knowledge of statistics, including the limits and pitfalls; ability to apply measurements and use results in decisions.
    - **Systems thinking**: The ability to see an organization as a system of interconnected elements organized to meet goals; to understand the interactions between these elements, how they influence each other, and the system as a whole.
    - **Visual thinking**: The ability to understand and interpret information conveyed through visualizations, such as graphs, charts, etc.
    - **Curiosity**: Ability to engage by asking meaningful questions driven by the desire to learn.
    - **Skepticism**: Willingness to question what one is seeing; to ensure one understands context and limitations of information.
    - **Ethical thinking**: Understanding the potential for good or harm that might come from the collection or use of data.
    - **Communication skills**: The ability to share insights with other people.

36. Some opportunities that can be implemented to use and manipulate data in day-to-day activities include:
    - Creating a spreadsheet to track the completion of steps in a workflow.
    - Querying data to answer a question.
    - Creating a form or spreadsheet to organize data for analysis.
    - Organizing data for a presentation.
    - Creating a set of data visualizations to explain a problem.
    - Evaluating the quality of data via data profiling.
    - Diagramming a data flow to identify risk points in the data chain.
    - Performing root cause analysis of a data issue.

Quality Management as the Context for DQ

Educational Objectives

Upon completion of this assignment, you should be able to:

1. Define terms related to data quality. Understand how they differ and combine to describe an approach to managing data.
2. Summarize the ideas of critical thought leaders in quality management who have significantly influenced data quality management:
   - **Shewhart**: Statistical Process Control and the Control Chart, Plan, Do, Check, Act.
   - **Deming**: System of Profound Knowledge and the 14 Points.
   - **Juran**: The Pareto Principle and Quality By Design.
   - **Ishikawa**: Quality Circles, Kaizen, and the Fishbone Diagram.
3. Describe concepts from product and service quality management that have been applied to data quality management through the work of data quality thought leaders:
   - **Richard Wang, Diane Strong, and the MIT Information Quality program**: Data as a product, Data Quality Dimensions from the data consumer point of view.
   - **Tom Redman**: Special properties of data and organizational politics of data.
   - **Larry English**: Total Information Quality Management, Data Stewardship.
   - **David Loshin**: The economic value of data; data and embedded knowledge.
   - **Danette McGilvray**: The Ten Steps process (applying process management to data quality problems); POSMAD, the data life cycle.

For each assignment, define or describe each of the Key Terms and Concepts and answer each of the Review and Discussion Questions.

Key Terms and Concepts

Data Quality:

Dimension of Quality:

Data Quality Management:

Data Quality Issue:

Data Standard:

Data Quality Improvement:

Data Life Cycle:

Data Supply Chain:

Review Questions

1. What is the core work of managing data quality? What are the top two goals? What is not a goal of managing data quality?

2. What do data quality dimensions do?

3. Identify the practices of data quality management.

4. Which of the following statements is true?

    A. Data standards can only be defined in relation to data structures or values.
    B. For insurance companies, some reporting requirements are considered standards since they must adhere to them to meet regulatory reporting requirements.
    C. Neither is true.
    D. Both are true.

5. Managing the quality of data requires answering what three questions?

6. What information is needed to define expectations for high-quality data?

7. What does it take to detect low-quality data?

8. What is required to take action when data does not meet expectations?

9. Shewhart identified two kinds of variation in the manufacturing process. Describe them.

10. What does it mean for a process to be in statistical control? How can Shewhart's concepts of variation be used to improve a process?

11. Shewhart's insights provided the beginnings of an approach to a true process improvement methodology. Identify the steps.

12. How does Shewhart's Statistical Process Control (SPC) use statistics?

13. Identify the value of the Shewhart Cycle and describe the phases.

14. List the four lenses through which leadership could view the world provided by Deming.

15. What are the characteristics that Juran identifies that help organizations succeed in quality improvement?

16. Identify the goals and steps of Juran's Quality Planning, Quality Control, and Quality Improvement.

17. What is Juran's definition of quality?

18. Identify some of the main points of Juran's Quality by Design.

19. What does Juran have to say about information, and how does that concept relate to metadata?

20. Identify and describe Ishikawa's main contributions to quality improvement.

21. Identify the six M's that classify factors in Ishikawa's fishbone diagram and identify how they can be applied to data management.

22. What other M do some analysts add to Ishikawa's factors? What does that include?

23. What is the major concept learned from the work of pioneers in the product quality?

24. List the set of principles derived from quality pioneers that support achieving a high-quality result.

25. Describe the four general categories of data quality identified by Wang and Strong.

26. Which of the following statements is not true?

    A. Wang and Strong present a process for developing high-quality information products that is analogous to product manufacture.

    B. According to Redman, technology should drive business to allow full use of the organization's data.

    C. English sees data as a product or organizational processes and as a resource that must be managed throughout its life cycle.

    D. All of the above.

27. List Redman's characteristics of high-quality data.

28. How does Redman go beyond the direct analogy between data and other products?

29. List Redman's special properties of data that shed light on how data differs from other products.

30. Identify the steps in English's improvement cycle.

31. How does English see the concept of data stewardship?

32. Which of the following statements is not true?

A. Loshin articulated the concepts of the economic value of data quality management and the relationship between enterprise knowledge and data.
B. Loshin's work shows the value of documenting information upfront when systems and processes are being developed, rather than having to mine the data to understand how the system itself works.
C. According to Loshin, there are only direct costs associated with poor-quality data whereas high-quality data has both direct and indirect benefits.
D. None of the above is true.

33. Identify the hard/direct and soft/indirect impacts of poor-quality data.

34. Describe Loshin's thoughts on the relationship between knowledge and data.

35. Describe McGilvray's Ten Step improvement cycle.

36. Identify McGilvray's POSMAD, a clear model of the data lifecycle.

37. What are the implications that can be derived from McGilvray's POSMAD?

Discussion Questions

NOTE: The questions below are intended to continue to challenge you to test your knowledge of the required reading by applying what you have studied to real-life situations.

No suggested answers are provided at the end of the assignment for these types of open discussion questions. Answers may vary by student and will depend on their organization's culture, resources, and processes.

1. Within your organization, which quality management thought leaders' ideas are in use?

2. Within your organization, which data quality management thought leader's ideas are in use?

3. How do you apply the data quality management ideas presented in this assignment in your work?

Answers to Assignment 3 Questions

NOTE: These answers are provided to give students a basic understanding of acceptable types of responses. They are often not the only valid answers and are not intended to provide an exhaustive response to the questions.

Key Terms and Concepts

Data Quality: A measure of the degree to which data fits the purposes of data consumers.

Dimension of Quality: A measurable characteristic of data, through which its quality can be understood, assessed, and quantified.

Data Quality Management: The application of quality management practices to data with the intent of ensuring that data is fit for the purposes of data consumers.

Data Quality Issue: Any obstacle to the use of data, regardless of its root cause(s) and regardless of how it can be resolved.

Data Standard: An assertion about how data should be created, presented, transformed, or conformed for purposes of consistency in presentation and meaning and to enable more efficient use.

Data Quality Improvement: A measurable positive change in data quality levels within an organization or process.

Data Life Cycle: A set of high-level phases that describe how data is created, maintained, used, and enhanced over time, and ultimately disposed of.

Data Supply Chain: A set of processes through which data is distributed and moved within an organization or between organizations.

Review Questions

1. The core work of managing data quality is taking the concept of data quality from an abstract idea to something that can be defined more objectively through the choices about measurement. The first goal of managing data quality is to ensure that data is in good enough condition to be used by data consumers. A secondary goal is to make data more usable and trustworthy from the perspective of the data consumer. Perfect data is not a goal.

2. Data dimensions provide ways to describe the degree to which data is fit for purpose. They are the means through which to reduce uncertainty around data quality to more concrete characteristics.

3. Practices of data quality management include:

   - Setting or adopting data standards and establishing data quality requirements.
   - Assessing data against standards and requirements.
   - Implementing controls to enforce and/or monitor data quality.

- Reporting on the results of assessments and monitoring so that data consumers are aware of quality levels and can make decisions about whether to use data based on this input.
- Managing data issues, ideally by eliminating the root causes of these issues.
- Acting on Improvement Opportunities. Proposing and implementing process and technical changes to prevent data issues, enforce data quality standards, and improve the overall trustworthiness of organizational data.

4. B. For insurance companies, some reporting requirements are considered standards since they must adhere to them to meet regulatory reporting requirements.

5. Managing the quality of data requires answering the three questions:

   - What is meant by high-quality data within this context?
   - How can low-quality data be detected?
   - What action should be taken when the data is not of high-enough quality?

6. To define expectations for high-quality data, the following information is needed:

   - Specific information in context about data production and usage.
   - Adopting the perspective of the data consumer by directly asking what they expect and require of the data.

7. Envisioning the multiple ways that things can go wrong with data collection, movement, and transformation is the first step in detecting low-quality data. Using this information to implement controls that prevent issues where possible and monitoring routines that detect undesirable or unexpected conditions when preventable controls are not an option.

8. When data does not meet expectations, the following is required:

   - Understanding of the impact of data issues on the organization and the ability to prioritize based on the costs of poor-quality data and the benefits of high-quality data.
   - The ability to act or escalate in a timely manner so as to limit the impact of data issues on organizational processes.

9. Shewhart's insight is that there are two kinds of variation in manufacturing processes:
   - Normal, unassignable, common cause variation inherent to the process.
   - Special cause or assignable cause variation due to factors outside the process. It is less predictable, impacting some output but not others, and may be intermittent.

10. A process is in "statistical control" if it is only influenced by common cause variation. If factors outside the process are influencing the results, the process is not in control. Processes can be evaluated for both common and special causes. Special cause variation can be eliminated and the impact of common cause variation can be reduced.

11. Shewhart's insights include:

    - Understand the process.
    - Measure the process.
    - Identify and eliminate special causes.
    - Reduce the effects of common cause variation.
    - Monitor to detect changes.

12. SPC uses measures of central tendency and measures of variability around a central tendency to set control limits for a stable process. Measures of central tendency – the mean, median, and mode – describe how values cluster around a central value. Measures of variation around central tendency – range, variance, and standard deviation – describe how spread-out the values are from a central value.

13. The Shewhart Cycle applies scientific thinking to process improvement. The phases are:
    - **PLAN**: Establish the goals or desired outcomes from the process.
    - **DO**: Execute the process according to the plan.
    - **CHECK**: Use measurements and observations to evaluate actual process outcomes against expected outcomes and goals.
    - **ACT**: Implement improvements.

14. According to Deming, leadership can view the world through the following lens:

    - An appreciation of a system in which you are working, including the organization in which you work, but also its suppliers, processes, and customers.
    - Understanding of variation within the system, including sources of variation on the impact of variation on quality.
    - Epistemology, or a theory of knowledge, as well as the limits of what can be known.
    - Psychology, or a theory of human nature, i.e., understanding how people work and recognizing that individuals are subject to the conditions of the system in which they work.

15. The characteristics that Juran identifies that help organizations succeed in quality improvement include:

    - Universal commitment to the goals.
    - A common language and unit of measure (money).
    - Training that reinforces goals and allows people to understand what is required to meet them.

16. The goals and steps of Juran's Quality Planning, Quality Control, and Quality Improvement include:

    The goal of quality planning is to develop products and processes to meet customers' needs. The steps are:
    - Establish quality goals.
    - Identify the customers and determine their needs.
    - Develop product features to meet these needs and processes to produce these features.
    - Establish process controls and transfer to operating forces.

    The goal of quality control is to monitor performance in relation to quality goals and act on the differences. The steps are:
    - Evaluate actual quality performance.
    - Compare actuals to goals.
    - Act on the difference.

    The goal of quality improvement is to raise the quality performance beyond the original quality goals. The steps are:
    - Establish the infrastructure needed to secure annual quality improvement.
    - Identify the specific needs for improvement, and set up improvement projects.
    - Establish project teams with clear responsibilities.
    - Provide resources, motivation, and training for teams to:
      - Diagnose the causes of poor quality.

    o   Stimulate the establishment of remedies.

    o   Establish controls to hold the gain.

17. According to Juran, quality products must possess desired characteristics and be free from defects.

18. Juran's Quality by Design:
    - Points to the need to plan for quality throughout the product development process.
    - Requires customer focus and customer input throughout the process.
    - Provides a unifying concept for the organization to understand the connection between planning, control, improvement, and high-quality outcomes.
    - Stresses the dual responsibility of those who plan to provide the features to meet customer needs and to provide the process to meet operational needs.

19. Juran points out that information, in the form of product documentation, is part of a high-quality product. Without this information, customers may not be successful using the product. A similar argument can be made about the connection between metadata and data. Metadata is a required component of any data product. Lack of metadata is a quality issue because it is an obstacle to data use.

20. Ishikawa's main contributions to quality improvement include:

    - Quality circles are groups of employees trained to look for, analyze, and propose solutions to work-related problems and to seek out opportunities for improvement.
    - Cause and effect diagram, known as the fishbone diagram, classifies factors contributing to general problems in order to assess how they affect a specific problem.

21. The six M's that classify factors in Ishikawa's fishbone diagram are:

    - Machine includes equipment and technology, which, for data management, would be technical architecture and software for developing applications.
    - Method involves the process steps and the clarity of the process definition. For data management, this would include requirements gathering, data modeling, and software development.
    - Manpower/mind power is the people working manually or mentally. For data management, this refers to whether people have the knowledge, skills, and experience to do the work in a way that meets quality requirements.
    - Materials include the raw material and information used to create the product. For data management, this includes knowledge of the input data (metadata, process information, quality assessment) and the requirements for the data product.
    - Milieu is the physical and cultural condition in which work is executed. For data management, this would include the relationship between business and IT.
    - Measurement is the inspection and feedback about the system process and other factors. For data management, this includes controls, quality assurance, and feedback from data consumers as part of user acceptance testing.

22. Management, which can include things like funding models and processes, management decision-making structure and system (command/control vs. bottom up), incentives for quality, recognition programs, and vision or purpose.

23. The work of these pioneers shows not only that it is possible to produce higher quality products and services, but that doing so reduces the costs associated with rework and customer dissatisfaction.

24. The set of principles derived from quality pioneers that support achieving a high-quality result are:

    - Quality requires commitment from leadership.
    - Quality requires engagement of staff.
    - Quality focuses on meeting customer requirements.
    - Set goals and measure against them.
    - Manage the production process.
    - Manage the supply chain.
    - Manage the product life cycle.
    - Continuously improve.

25. Wang and Strong's four general categories of data quality are:

    - **Intrinsic DQ:** The extent to which data values are in conformance with the actual or true values. Intrinsically good data is accurate, correct, and objective, and comes from a reputable source. Associated data quality dimensions are accuracy, objectivity, believability, and reputation.
    - **Contextual DQ:** The extent to which data is applicable (pertinent) to the task of the data user. Contextually appropriate data must be relevant to the consumer, in terms of timeliness and completeness. Associated data quality dimensions are value-added, relevancy, timeliness, completeness, and an appropriate amount of data.
    - **Representational DQ:** The extent to which data is presented in an intelligible and clear manner (represented concisely and consistently) so that the consumer is able to interpret the data. Associated data quality dimensions are interpretability, ease of understanding, representational consistency, and concise representation.
    - **Accessibility DQ:** Emphasizes the importance of the role of systems; understood as the extent to which data is available to or obtainable by the data consumer. The system must also be secure. Dimensions include accessibility and access security. Associated data quality dimensions are accessibility and access security.

26. B. According to Redman, technology should drive business to allow full use of the organization's data.

27. Redman's characteristics of high-quality data are:

    - Fit for purpose.
    - Free from defects.
    - Possessing desired features.
    - The Customer is the final arbiter of quality.
    - Quality requires context – what is high quality for one purpose may not be high quality for another purpose.

28. Data is a unique source of competitive advantage, which is tied directly to the special properties of data itself. Organizational data cannot be purchased or replaced, and nothing can be substituted for it.

29. Redman's special properties of data that shed light on how data differs from other products are:

    - Data multiply.
    - Data is more complex than it appears.
    - Data and information have become the language of business, subtle, nuanced, and often unique.
    - Data and information create value when used.
    - Data and information are organic, changing to suit different uses.

- Data and information are not consumed with use.
- Data is a meta-asset.
- Data and information are intangible.
- Each organization's data and information are unique, so investment in data is an investment in competitive advantage.

30. The steps in English's improvement cycle are:

- **Assess data definition and the information architecture quality**: Determine whether knowledge workers have the information they need to understand and use data and information.
- **Assess information quality and the information architecture quality**: Measure information against characteristics like accuracy and completeness.
- **Measure non-quality costs and risks**: Define a business case, based on process failures, scrap and rework, and lost opportunity.
- **Re-engineer and correct data**: Reengineering is intended to address the root causes of data quality problems and prevent them from recurring.
- **Improve information process quality**: Apply the PDCA cycle to processes that create and transform data.
- **Establish the information quality environment**: Adopt the set of practices that create the context required for Total Quality Management, which includes people, processes, and technology.

31. English advocates the idea of data stewardship as a critical "people" component of the information environment, defined as the willingness to be accountable for a set of business information for the well-being of the larger organization by operating in service, rather than in control, of those around us. Stewardship is a set of accountabilities.

32. C. According to Loshin, there are only direct costs associated with poor-quality data whereas high-quality data has both direct and indirect benefits.

33. The hard/direct and soft/indirect impacts of poor-quality data are:

- Direct/Hard impacts
  - Detection and correction of data errors
  - Scrap and rework
  - Operational delays
  - Customer attrition.
- Indirect/Soft impacts
  - Difficulty in decision-making
  - Organizational conflict
  - Public relations efforts / "spin".

34. Knowledge is embedded in the processes designed to collect and report data, often so deeply embedded that those using the process may not be fully aware of it. When this happens, the process needs to be reverse engineered to understand the drivers and assumptions behind the data and to articulate them to determine if they are still valid. Assumptions about the quality of the data must be included: which fields are optional and which are mandatory, which are related to each other, and how objects are designed to interact.

35. McGilvray's Ten Step improvement cycle:

- **Step 1, Determine business needs and approach**: Get a clear picture of the goals of the project and the best ways to meet them; identify ways poor-quality data can be an obstacle to reaching business goals.
- **Step 2, Analyze the information environment**: Look at conditions and situations that create or exacerbate data quality problems.
- **Step 3, Assess data quality and Step 4, Assess business impact**: Together these steps involve clarifying, defining, and quantifying issues, obstacles, or requirements and understanding the impact on business processes and stakeholders' goals.
- **Step 5, Determine root causes of data issues and Step 6, Develop improvement plans**: Identify the causes beyond the immediate symptoms (root causes) and prevent issues from recurring based on the results from steps 3 and 4.
- **Step 7, Prevent future data errors and Step 8, Correct current data errors**: Envision what can go wrong with the data and use the process of correcting data for insights into the kinds of controls that will be most effective in preventing the errors.
- **Step 9, Monitor controls**: Ensure that data quality remains in range and take appropriate action when it does not.
- **Step 10, Communicate, manage, and engage people throughout**: Share appropriate, clear, and effective communications at every step of the process, recognizing that the means of communication may differ based on the size and complexity of the project.

36. McGilvray's POSMAD, a clear model of the data lifecycle:

- **Plan**: Anything done to a project before going into production to solve the problem.
- **Obtain**: Acquire or create data for use; a simple or complex effort which may include data from internal sources, external sources, or a combination.
- **Store/Share**: Maybe be processes that store and distribute data in electronic form or hardcopy.
- **Maintain**: Ensure the resource works properly, which includes updates, changes, and/or manipulations.
- **Apply**: Use the resource to meet goals.
- **Dispose**: Delete resource when it is no longer useful; data may be archived or destroyed.

37. The implications derived from McGilvray's POSMAD include:

- Different management is needed at different points in the life cycle.
- All phases have costs.
- Value is gained only in the Apply phase.
- High quality depends on good management at every phase.

Data Quality Dimensions

Educational Objectives

Upon completion of this assignment, you should be able to:

1. Understand what data quality dimensions are and how they can be used.
2. Review a framework for data quality dimensions that accounts for data attributes, entities, and sets.
3. Understand how the quality of the data environment – the data model, metadata, reference data, master data, system reliability – can be understood through dimensions of quality.
4. Understand how dimensions can be used to assess, monitor, and report on data quality.

For each assignment, define or describe each of the Key Terms and Concepts and answer each of the Review and Discussion Questions.

Key Terms and Concepts

Accurate:

Complete:

Consistent with Business Rules:

Current/Timely:

Accessible:

Relevant:

Column or Field:

Format Correctness:

Domain of Values:

Validity:

Dataset:

Data Domain Integrity:

Data Value Integrity:

Integrity of Related Fields:

Parent/Child Referential Integrity:

Child/Parent Referential Integrity:

System Reconciliation:

Reasonability:

Data Model:

Metadata:

Business Metadata:

Technical Metadata:

Operational Metadata:

Reference Data:

Master Data:

Entity Resolution:

False Positives:

False Negatives:

Review Questions

1. List the fundamental, measurable data quality dimensions that characterize fit-for-purpose data.

2. What is the purpose of data quality dimensions?

3. What two ideas must be accounted for in order to use data quality dimensions?

4. List the dimensions of data quality. For each, identify the data structures (data field, dataset/entity, metadata, reference data, and master data management) for which it is an important component of data quality.

5. What does completeness mean when applied at the field level?

6. What roles do business rules, process requirements, and technical requirements play in defining completeness?

7. How can completeness be measured for fields?

8. Identify some considerations for assessing format correctness.

9. True or False: When a field has a unique acceptable format, data entry instructions are the only way to constrain the data to fit the format.

10. What does accuracy mean when applied to a field?

11. Why is field accuracy so difficult to measure? What conditions make it more difficult to measure accuracy for transformed data?

12. True or False: If data is accurate, then questions about validity and format correctness are moot.

13. Identify concerns for field validity.

14. Can field validity be measured?

15. What does consistency mean when applied to fields, and how is this recognized?

16. How can field consistency be measured?

17. What does completeness mean at the dataset level?

18. True or False: Completeness at the dataset level is independent of completeness at the column level.

19. True or False: You cannot meet the non-duplication of data criteria unless you clearly define what constitutes an entity instance and what constitutes a unique record.

20. How is currency maintained in a dataset?

21. How is currency enforced? What role do service level agreements play in enforcement?

22. What does it mean for datasets to have integrity?

23. True or False: With respect to the integrity of related fields, if the fields are part of the same object, this can be considered a validity measure.

24. How can system reconciliation be defined?

25. How is consistency defined at the dataset level and how does it differ from integrity?

26. True or False: Consistent datasets will have the same number of records.

27. How does reasonability connect to consistency and how is it measured?

28. True or False: Although metadata, reference data, and master data are categories of data, dimensions of data do not apply to them.

29. What are some characteristics of data models?

30. How carefully data is modeled and implemented can affect the ability to use the data? Identify some factors related to modeling that can make it easier to use data.

31. What is the goal of Master Data Management (MDM) and how is this goal achieved?

32. True or False: The design, maintenance, and operation of IT systems do not have any impact on the quality of the data they make available.

33. What are the characteristics of highly reliable systems?

34. Documentation for a highly reliable system means:

35. To be predictable, a highly reliable system must meet what criteria?

36. What does it mean that a system is accountable?

37. What does it mean for a system to be controlled?

38. True or False: Highly reliable systems capture information about their processes so that overall performance can be monitored and so that the system can be audited.

39. What security controls are in place for a highly reliable system?

40. How do data dimensions provide a common language around expectations and issues related to data quality?

Discussion Questions

NOTE: The questions below are intended to continue to challenge you to test your knowledge of the required reading by applying what you have studied to real-life situations.

No suggested answers are provided at the end of the assignment for these types of open discussion questions. Answers may vary by student and will depend on their organization's culture, resources, and processes.

1. Describe some of the data dimensions used by your organization.

2. How are these dimensions used to control the processes?

3. What was the process for defining the data dimensions? Who was involved?

4. How are metrics communicated throughout your organization?

Answers to Assignment 4 Questions

NOTE: These answers are provided to give students a basic understanding of acceptable types of responses. They are often not the only valid answers and are not intended to provide an exhaustive response to the questions.

Key Terms and Concepts

Accurate: The information correctly represents what it purports to represent; i.e., it does not contain errors.

Complete: All records required for the purpose are available and fully populated.

Consistent with Business Rules: Data values within and between records are coherent based on the business process they represent.

Current/Timely: The information is up-to-date for the purpose.

Accessible: The information must be available for use in decisions and other actions.

Relevant: The data must be able to answer questions that people are asking of it.

Column or Field: Represents an attribute, a single characteristic of an entity.

Format Correctness: Measures the degree to which data conforms to the format requirements as documented in business process requirements or other standards and formalized in a data model.

Domain of Values: A list of values in a data dictionary, a value in a code table, a range or minimum and maximum values, or results of a calculation or business rule.

Validity: Refers to the degree to which data values are part of a defined domain of values.

Dataset: A collection of data brought together for a particular purpose, including tables, all the objects in a given system, or all the objects in a data domain.

Data Domain Integrity: The domain of valid values is the same for all instances of a logical attribute across different datasets.

Data Value Integrity: The populated values for all instances of the same attribute for the same entity instance at a given time are the exact same value across datasets.

Integrity of Related Fields: The populated values on related fields between datasets are in a valid relationship with each other.

Parent/Child Referential Integrity: Where there is a foreign key relationship between two objects, each record in the child table should have a corresponding record in the parent table.

Child/Parent Referential Integrity: Where there is a foreign key relationship between two objects and a population rule that requires a child record, then each record in the parent table should have a corresponding record in the child table.

System Reconciliation: Data within a downstream system is expected to reconcile with its direct sources and/or with the systems of record for the data.

Reasonability: The degree to which data corresponds to known facts.

Data Model: A depiction of an organization's data. that uses symbols and text formally and precisely to represent an organization's data, data requirements, and some combination of these.

Metadata: Describes what data an organization has, where it is located, what it means, where it originated, how it can and cannot be used, how it is processed, when it was updated, how it needs to be protected, who can access and use it, and so on.

Business Metadata: Focuses on information required to use data in operations and analytics.

Technical Metadata: Focuses on physical characteristics of data and requirements around technical aspects of moving and accessing data.

Operational Metadata: Describes details of how data is processed, and how the system is maintained.

Reference Data: Used to characterize other data in an organization or to relate data to information beyond the bounds of the organization.

Master Data: Represents entities that matter most to an organization, such as those logged in transactions, reported on, measured, and analyzed.

Entity Resolution: The use of matching logic to bring together records from different sources and link them through identifiers that enable their use in multiple systems.

False Positives: Records that appear to represent the same entity but do not.

False Negatives: Records that appear not to represent the same entity but do.

Review Questions

1. The fundamental, measurable data quality dimensions that characterize fit-for-purpose data are:
    - Accurate/Correct.
    - Complete.
    - Consistent with Business Rules.
    - Current/Timely.
    - Accessible.
    - Relevant.

2. Data quality dimensions are the means by which we reduce the abstraction around data quality to more concrete characteristics.

3. The two ideas that must be accounted for in order to use data quality dimensions are:
    - The things we want to know about.
    - The characteristics we want to know about them.

4. Dimensions of data quality and the data structures important to each are:
    - Completeness: data field, dataset/entity, metadata, references data, master data management (MDM).

- Format Correctness: data field.
- Accuracy: data field, MDM.
- Validity: data field.
- Consistency: data field, dataset/entity.
- Currency: dataset/entity, metadata, reference data.
- Non-Duplication: dataset/entity.
- Integrity: dataset/entity.
- Reasonability: dataset/entity.
- Clarity: metadata, references data.
- Accessibility: metadata, reference data, master data management (MDM).
- Precision/Granularity: reference data.

5. Completeness refers to the degree to which required data is present. Mandatory data must be populated with a non-default value. Optional fields must be populated based on business rules that describe the conditions of the population.

6. Business rules and process requirements identify which fields are mandatory and which are optional. Technical requirements relate to optionality, although these do not always reflect business expectations. Some fields may be considered optional from a technical standpoint, but are required for the business purpose.

7. Completeness can be measured:
   - For mandatory fields, the ratio of rows with a non-default value to the total number of rows. Users can determine what ratio makes the data usable.
   - For optional fields, measurements must account for the business rules that describe when a field must be populated.

8. Some data has clear format constraints. However, there can be concerns about how to store data.
   - Should numbers be stored with leading zeros?
   - How should a field consisting of numbers, but not used in calculations, be stored as text or a number?
   - Should a field composed of a number and an alphanumeric character (e.g., SSN and dates) be stored with the non-numeric character? That is, should the SSN include the '-' or should dates include the "/"?

9. False. Technical constraints, e.g., edits, can be put in place to force compliance.

10. Accuracy refers to the degree to which data values correctly represent their real-world counterparts. This is true for reported data as well as transformed data.

11. Accuracy is difficult to measure since it is usually not possible to compare the data to the real-world counterpart. For transformed data, logic should be sound and account for all logical possibilities; this should be tested during development of the transformation.

12. True.

13. Field validity concerns include:
    - Validity can be extended across multiple fields, so relationships must be checked.
    - Data may be valid but inaccurate.

14. As with completeness, validity can be measured by the percentage of records with valid data. It is also important to ensure that the complete domain of values is clearly defined in a form that enables

measurements to be taken. Users determine whether the percentage of valid records makes the data usable.

15. Field consistency refers to the degree to which data follows expected patterns. At the column level, patterns are recognized through frequency distributions of values.

16. Field consistency is measured by applying techniques of Statistical Process Control (SPC), which involves comparing the frequency distribution of any new increment of data to the historical distribution using measures of central tendency (mean, median, mode).

17. Completeness at the dataset level means:
    - The dataset contains all the attributes required to make it relevant and usable.
    - All the required records are in the dataset. i.e., all records related to a specific population, all records generated during a set timeframe, all records from a specific system, or a combination of all these conditions.

18. False. If the column level is not complete, the dataset is not complete.

19. True.

20. For a system that keeps only one record for each instance and updates the record as values change, each field should contain the most recent value for the attribute. For a system that maintains historical data, each record should show a timeframe and the value that existed during that timeframe.

21. For data stores that contain historical data, the update process should be automated and include audit fields that indicate when data has changed. Service level agreements ensure that consumers are aware of the enforcement.

22. Datasets that have integrity should be measurably the same, though measurements can be taken at different levels depending on how the datasets are structured.

23. True.

24. Depending on the structure of the systems, reconciliation can be defined by the number of records, the number of represented entities, and reconciliation between amount fields. In cases where records are excluded during data processing, reconciliation logic will need to account for the records.

25. At the dataset level, consistency refers to the equivalence of the related datasets. Integrity implies that exact reconciliation is expected, while consistency implies only similarity is expected.

26. False. Depending on the structural differences, the datasets may not have the same number of records. In fact, exact correspondence is not expected.

27. Reasonability is connected to consistency since it requires a baseline against which to be measured. Measures of reasonability can be informed by column consistency.

28. False. Data dimensions do apply to them, and to be of high quality, these must be complete, accurate, accessible, usable, and trustworthy.

29. Characteristics of data models include:
    - Data models use symbols and text formally and precisely to represent an organization's data, its data requirements, or some combination of these.

- Data models may be created with different levels of detail (conceptual, logical, physical) depending on their purpose.
- One goal of the model is to document unambiguous expectations about the data, thus enabling communication and education of those expectations.

30. Factors related to modeling that can make it easier to use data include:
    - Consistent naming conventions within an application/across systems.
    - Consistent use of default values within an application/across systems.
    - Appropriate degree of precision for numeric fields.
    - Consistent formatting of similar fields within an application/across systems.
    - Clear correspondence between field names, definitions, and actual data.
    - Limited redundancy of data (duplicate or similar columns) within an application.

31. The goal of MDM is to create a single source of truth. This is achieved through a process of entity resolution, which links records together.

32. False: How IT systems are designed, maintained, and operated has an impact on the data they make available.

33. The characteristics of highly reliable systems are:
    - Documented and supported.
    - Predictable.
    - Accountable.
    - Controlled.
    - Transparent/auditable.
    - Secure.

34. Documentation for a highly reliable system means:
    - Users understand the purpose of the system and enough of the design to have confidence in it.
    - Training is available.
    - Users have a way to ask questions.

35. To be predictable, a highly reliable system must have a data delivery schedule in place that is monitored to ensure that the schedule is met.

36. A system is accountable when service level agreements (SLA) are in place to define when the system will make data available to data consumers, and data consumers are informed when SLAs are broken.

37. A system is controlled when system edits are in place to prevent the creation of low-quality data. Automated controls are in place, and processes are monitored to ensure performance and availability.

38. True.

39. The security controls in place for a highly reliable system include:
    - Enable legitimate access and prevent inappropriate access to the system.
    - Prevent unauthorized uses of specific datasets.
    - Prevent unauthorized changes to data.

40. Data dimensions provide logical categories for reporting and can be used for individual and aggregate metrics. These metrics clarify the level of data quality for different uses.

The Dynamics of Data Quality Management

Educational Objectives

Upon completion of this assignment, you should be able to:

1. Describe the data life cycle and how knowledge of the data life cycle can be used to help manage and govern data more effectively.
2. Describe the Data Supply Chain and its impact on data quality.
3. Describe the Data Quality Improvement Cycle and the insight it provides for data management as a whole.
4. Describe the core functions of data quality management and how they interact. These include: setting data standards; assessing data quality; implementing monitoring controls; reporting on data quality; managing data issues; and acting on process improvement opportunities.
5. Describe how these models (Data Life Cycle, Data Supply Chain, and Data Quality Improvement Cycle) interact and inform decisions about how to manage data quality within an insurance organization.

For each assignment, define or describe each of the Key Terms and Concepts and answer each of the Review and Discussion Questions.

Key Terms and Concepts

Planning:

Create/Obtain:

Design and Enable:

Store and Share:

Maintaining:

Using and Applying:

Gather and Utilize Feedback:

Enhancing and Improving:

Disposing:

Data Supply Chain:

Data Lineage:

Data Quality Improvement Cycle:

Review Questions

1. Identify the phases of the data life cycle.

2. How does planning cover the entire data life cycle?

3. Few companies create new processes to produce new data, but what should they do when new products or services are introduced?

4. What features should the design and enable phase of the data life cycle account for?

5. How does the store and share phase of the data life cycle support data quality?

6. Which of the following statements is not true regarding the maintenance phase of the data life cycle?

    A. Maintenance is important in situations where data moves from an administrative system to analytic data stores.
    B. Maintenance processes should be associated with quality requirements.
    C. Maintenance processes do not require metadata.
    D. All of the above are true.

7. Which of the following is true of the use/apply phase of the data life cycle?

    A. This is the only life cycle phase during which the organization gets value from the data.
    B. This is the only phase that supports data usage.
    C. This phase is the least important source of feedback about the quality of data.
    D. All of the above are true.

8. Which of the following is true of the questions raised in the feedback phase of the data life cycle?

A. Questions of the ability to use the data may identify limitations on the data structure, as well as the data itself.
B. Questions on the quality of data may point to process improvements through issue remediation and new data requirements.
C. Questions on the meaning of data can provide an opportunity to improve metadata.
D. All of the above are true.

9. Identify some ways that data enhancement can occur.

10. True or False: Data enhancements require a new round of planning and creation/obtaining phases, but other phases of the data life cycle are not needed.

11. How does knowledge of the data life cycle help manage data quality?

12. How is a typical insurance Data Supply Chain complicated?

13. What is the focus of the Data Supply Chain, and how does this help identify and resolve data quality issues? How can it be presented?

14. Which of the following statements is not true?

    A. The Data Supply Chain tracks data lineage.
    B. Unlike a physical supply chain, the Data Supply Chain doesn't include information on the costs of data and getting it to those who need it.
    C. By understanding the Data Supply Chain, data managers are better able to manage the organization's data.
    D. All of the above are false.

15. Identify the two components of actively managing for quality data.

16. Identify the core functions of a data quality management plan.

17. True or False: Insurance data managers must be concerned with both internal and external data standards.

18. Which of the following is true about data assessment?

    A. Assessment enables quantification of data quality.
    B. Assessment activities include data profiling and root cause analysis at each point of the data chain, but not necessarily between different points.
    C. Assessment describes the characteristics of specific data.
    D. All of the above are true.

19. True or False: The sole purpose of controls is to prevent errors.

20. Why is reporting the results of assessments and monitoring critical?

21. Managing data issues includes all of the following activities except:

    A. Identifying, quantifying, and prioritizing the causes of obstacles to data use.
    B. Facilitating the remediation of obstacles to data use, especially by eliminating the root causes.
    C. Reporting to data consumers the results of analyses.
    D. None of the above are activities used to manage data issues.

22. What is the goal of acting on improvement opportunities, and how is this core function implemented?

23. Identify some characteristics of a data quality improvement cycle.

24. Which of the following statements is not true of implementing a data quality improvement process?

    A. Activities should be facilitated and coordinated by people with knowledge and experience in data quality management or another improvement methodology.
    B. Activities should be coordinated since they impact both project and operational processes.
    C. Development teams have the experience and training to lead these activities.
    D. All of the above are not true.

25. Which of the following is true of the Data Life Cycle?

    A. The Data Life Cycle describes how a dataset will be managed over time.
    B. The Data Life Cycle accounts for the original set up of data.
    C. The Data Life Cycle supports data use through metadata, training, and user support.
    D. All of the above are true.

26. How does understanding the Data Life Cycle help organizations improve data quality?

27. How does the Data Supply Chain enable people to see and understand relationships between datasets and between different parts of the organization?

28. How do the Data Life Cycle and Data Supply Chain work together to support data quality?

29. How does an understanding of the Data Life Cycle and Data Supply Chain support managing the quality of data?

Discussion Questions

NOTE: The questions below are intended to continue to challenge you to test your knowledge of the required reading by applying what you have studied to real-life situations.

No suggested answers are provided at the end of the assignment for these types of open discussion questions. Answers may vary by student and will depend on their organization's culture, resources, and processes.

1. Does your organization use the data life cycle to manage and govern data? If so, how? If not, how could it be used to improve data quality in your organization?

2. How is the Data Supply Chain documented and used in your organization?

3. How is the Data Quality Improvement Cycle implemented in your organization?

4. Describe how the data life cycle, Data Supply Chain, and Data Quality Improvement Cycle work (or could work) to improve data quality in your organization.

Answers to Assignment 5 Questions

NOTE: These answers are provided to give students a basic understanding of acceptable types of responses. They are often not the only valid answers and are not intended to provide an exhaustive response to the questions.

Key Terms and Concepts

Planning: Data life cycle phase that includes defining expectations and requirements for quality and putting in motion the activities required to use the data over time.

Create/Obtain: Data life cycle phase that includes getting the required data, either by sourcing it through an existing process, purchasing it, or establishing a process to create it.

Design and Enable: Data life cycle phase that includes defining the technical and business processes that ensure data meets business requirements, including data quality requirements.

Store and Share: Data life cycle phase that involves putting data into a system that is secure and accessible to those who are authorized to see it and use it.

Maintaining: Data life cycle phase that includes implementing operational processes to keep data current.

Using and Applying: Data life cycle phase that includes sharing data to support operational processes, using data in analytics and reporting, and interpreting data to answer questions and solve problems.

Gather and Utilize Feedback: Data life cycle phase that focuses on the meaning of the data, the quality of the data, and the ability to use the data.

Enhancing and Improving: Data life cycle phase that includes both recognizing gaps and accounting for new requirements.

Disposing: Data life cycle phase that entails removing it from systems and processes based on regulatory requirements, contractual obligations, business requirements, or a combination of these things.

Data Supply Chain: Focuses on how particular datasets (each of which will have its own life cycle) move into and through an organization, thus enabling an understanding of the relationships between functions that create and use data.

Data Lineage: A type of metadata that describes where data originates and how it moves through an organization's systems and processes, and importantly, how it is transformed as it moves.

Data Quality Improvement Cycle: Provides a model and methodology for activities required to build awareness and make decisions about where to apply resources to increase data value.

Review Questions

1. The phases of the data life cycle are:

   - Plan/Prepare.
   - Create/Obtain.
   - Design and Enable.
   - Store and Share.
   - Maintain.
   - Use/Apply.
   - Gather and Utilize Feedback.
   - Enhance and Improve.
   - Dispose of.

2. Planning covers the entire data life cycle in the following ways:

   - Determines what data is needed in the requirements phase.
   - Identifies an approach by envisioning how requirements will be met and how data will be obtained, accessed, and maintained.
   - Supports use with the knowledge of known use cases, metadata management, training, and customer support.
   - Supports ongoing operations with access, maintenance, archival, and disposal requirements.
   - Defines criteria for quality, error prevention, and quality enforcement requirements.

3. At the beginning of the process, they should account not only for the data that will be created but also for how data will be collected, as well as what characteristics will make the dataset of high quality and provide this information to data suppliers.

4. The design and enable phase of the data life cycle should account for the following features:

   - Business processes that create data.
   - Business processes that use data.
   - The technology that executes these processes.
   - Controls that prevent data issues and enforce quality requirements.
   - Enterprise view of data.

5. Storage has a direct impact on the people and processes that access data, and as such, should be well documented and standardized as much as possible. The choices about storage also support security and privacy concerns.

6. C. Maintenance processes do need metadata to allow data consumers to understand when data is created, when it is updated, and when it is available for use.

7. A. All phases support data usage. This phase provides the most feedback regarding quality.

8. D.

9. When using data, people identify gaps in data, metadata, or in the tools used to access the data. Evolution of the business, either processes or compliance requirements, as well as technology changes, can lead to data enhancement.

10. False. Data enhancement requires the entire data life cycle to be restarted.

11. Understanding the overall data life cycle:
    - Enables the organization to build data quality and management activities required at different points in the life cycle.
    - Helps develop a clearer picture of the data supply chain.
    - Helps reduce risks related to data movement and sharing.
    - Answers questions about the value of enhancing data.

12. Once created, data in the insurance supply chain is used for multiple purposes, from marketing to claims administration to policy administration. Core insurance functions, such as underwriting, claims administration, actuarial, accounting, sales, and marketing, create data that is heterogeneous. Yet, this data is expected to fit together for management and reporting purposes.

13. The Data Supply Chain focuses on where data is created, moved, and used. It also identifies the purpose of the data. This is a way to identify data quality expectations, especially when data has multiple uses and requirements differ across those uses. Documentation of the Data Supply Chain, presented in architectural diagrams, data flows, and mapping documentation, is critical to identifying root causes of data issues and understanding their impact.

14. B. The Data Supply Chain provides information on costs associated with data.

15. Two components of actively managing for quality data are:
    - Focusing on organizational and cultural awareness: communication and training to raise awareness of the interconnectedness of the organization's data.
    - Focusing attention on a data quality improvement plan.

16. The core functions of a data quality management plan include:

    - Setting or adopting data standards and establishing data quality requirements.
    - Assessing data against standards and requirements.
    - Implementing controls to enforce and/or monitor data quality.
    - Reporting on the results of assessments and monitoring.
    - Managing data issues.
    - Acting on improvement opportunities.

17. True.

18. A.

19. False. Controls can also be used to monitor data and detect unexpected conditions or changes to data quality measures.

20. Reporting is critical to ensuring that data consumers' requirements are understood and met. They allow consumers to make decisions about whether to use the data based on the reported results.

21. C.

22. The goal of acting on improvement opportunities is to improve data quality. It is accomplished by proposing and driving the implementation of process and technical changes to prevent data errors, enforce data quality standards, and improve the overall trustworthiness of the organizational data.

23. Characteristics of a data quality improvement cycle include:
    - Improvement efforts can start at any point in the cycle.
    - Issues can be identified through assessments, monitoring, reporting, or by data consumers.

- Addressing data issues requires assessment and quantification of impact.
- The process may lead to insights that clarify requirements and standard definition.
- Capabilities can be applied individually or together at different levels: individual systems, datasets, entities, or attributes.
- Capabilities can be applied within functional business areas, across the data supply chain, and at different points in the data life cycle.

24. C. Development teams are not the best leaders.

25. D.

26. The Data Life Cycle helps the organization:

- Make better decisions about how to obtain, organize, store, and enable access to data.
- Avoid risks associated with data.

- Benefit data producers and consumers by requiring the creation and management of metadata and other forms of knowledge about data.

27. The supply chain:

- Depicts the details that bind the organization processes together by detailing process dependencies and multiple data uses.
- Identifies connection points that can represent data hazards, including costs and delays.
- Identifies data gaps and inconsistencies.

28. Knowledge of both enables the organization to manage both individual datasets and the relationships between them over time. This knowledge supports changes as requirements and demands for data evolve.

29. Life Cycle requirements can directly affect quality and the perception of quality, especially requirements for storage and maintenance. Metadata management is more effective if it is created early in the life cycle. The differences between systems are contributing factors to data issues. A driver for data standards is the need to ensure that data from different systems and processes along the data chain can be shared and integrated.

Data Quality and Standards

Educational Objectives

Upon completion of this assignment, you should be able to:

1. Explain the general importance of standards in identifying measurable criteria for assessing the quality of data.
2. Explain the context of the development of standards within the insurance industry, in response to regulatory requirements, and how these connect with data quality requirements.
3. Understand and describe the focus of different types of standards related to insurance processes and the form and content of insurance data. For example:
    a. Data content standards, like those issued by ACORD and ISO.
    b. Technical standards, like Electronic Data Interchange.
    c. Process standards, like Actuarial Standard of Practice No. 23: Data Quality.
    d. Standards for specific quality levels, as defined in the NAIC Statistical Handbook.
4. Describe how dimensions of quality can be used to develop standards that align with the expectations of regulators, as well as stakeholders along the internal supply chain.

For each assignment, define or describe each of the Key Terms and Concepts and answer each of the Review and Discussion Questions.

Key Terms and Concepts

Standard:

The Association for Cooperative Operations Research and Development (ACORD):

The International Association of Industrial Accident Boards and Commissions (IAIABC):

Workers Compensation Insurance Organizations (WCIO):

Workgroup for Electronic Data Interchange (WEDI):

Content Standards:

Technical Standards:

Electronic Data Interchange (EDI):

Process Standards:

Quality Standards for Specific Reporting Data:

Statistical Agents:

Review Questions

1. What is the purpose of establishing data standards?

2. Why are standards important in the insurance industry and what role do they play?

3. Insurance depends on the successful transfer of different kinds of information. What types of entities might share insurance data?

4. Why is it beneficial for insurance companies to conform to standards developed by industry associations?

5. What conditions does ACORD identify as reasons why data standards are of particular importance in the insurance industry? How do standards support the industry under these conditions?

6. Describe the focus areas of state regulation and the data requirements for each.

7. Why is compliance with regulation so complicated?

8. Identify the organizations that help mitigate the effects of regulatory compliance.

9. True or False: Insurers are only subject to federal and state regulation that directly affects the insurance industry and its products.

10. List the federal, state, and international regulations to which insurers are subjected.

11. What is the intent and major provisions of HIPAA?

12. Identify the five rules of HIPAA's Title II related to administrative simplification. Briefly describe their purpose.

13. What is the focus of the Gramm-Leach-Bliley Act of 1999 (GLBA)?

14. How does GLBA extend protection for private information?

15. What does the U.S. PATRIOT Act allow financial institutions and governmental agencies to do?

16. How does Data Quality Management allow for the identification of potentially concerning financial or terrorist activities?

17. What is the purpose of the Sarbanes-Oxley Act of 2002 (SOX)? How does SOX have an effect on data quality?

18. What are the main points addressed by President Biden's October 2022 executive order on safe, secure, and trustworthy artificial intelligence?

19. What is the purpose of the European Union's General Data Protection Regulation (GDPR)? What are some of the main protections provided by GDPR?

20. Standards outlined in regulations are not exactly data standards. Why do we consider them in a data management assignment?

21. In the 1980's, Insurance Services Office (ISO) and the National Council on Compensation Insurance (NCCI) adopted data element standards to improve the consistency and quality of data. List some of those standards.

22. True or False: Technical standards apply to formal requirements for files, fields, or delivery mechanisms that allow an organization to use internal data with limited data preparation work.

23. EDI standards are designed to enable data sharing through the concept of data interoperability. What are the technical requirements needed to support data interoperability?

24. What is the intention of the Actuarial Standard of Practice No. 23?

25. Why is the Actuarial Standard of Practice No. 23 considered a process standard?

26. What kinds of standards might be used for quality standards for specific data reporting?

27. Why is the NAIC Statistical Handbook considered a quality standard for reporting data?

28. How does financial data differ from statistical data?

29. Why are statistical agents who develop statistical plans considered a quality standard for reporting data?

30. True or False: The NAIC Statistical Handbook describes the standard of reporting for individual insurance companies but does not define standards for statistical agents.

31. Briefly describe the dimensions of quality and core data management practices addressed in the NAIC Handbook.

32. How can the relationship between insurers, statistical agents, and regulators be understood?

Discussion Questions

NOTE: The questions below are intended to continue to challenge you to test your knowledge of the required reading by applying what you have studied to real-life situations.

No suggested answers are provided at the end of the assignment for these types of open discussion questions. Answers may vary by student and will depend on their organization's culture, resources, and processes.

1. Discuss your company's interaction with statistical agents and other standard organizations. How do these organizations support data quality management in your company?

2. What describes your company's use of data standards? What is the structure to support them?

Answers to Assignment 6 Questions

NOTE: These answers are provided to give students a basic understanding of acceptable types of responses. They are often not the only valid answers and are not intended to provide an exhaustive response to the questions.

Key Terms and Concepts

Standard: A document that provides requirements, specifications, guidelines, or characteristics that can be used consistently to ensure that materials, products, processes, and services are fit for their purpose.

The Association for Cooperative Operations Research and Development (ACORD): An industry group that develops standards and describes the benefits of data standards within insurance.

The International Association of Industrial Accident Boards and Commissions (IAIABC): An international association of workers' compensation jurisdictional agencies and private organizations

Workers Compensation Insurance Organizations (WCIO): A voluntary, not-for-profit association of workers' compensation Data Collection Organizations

Workgroup for Electronic Data Interchange (WEDI): Develops standards related to the exchange and interoperability of health care data

Content Standards: Describe what data elements are required for reporting about a process and its outcomes.

Technical Standards: Describe the technical state the data must be in to be used as input for a process.

Electronic Data Interchange (EDI): The idea that organizations and sub-parts of organizations should be able to exchange information through electronic means without the need for human intervention during the process.

Process Standards: Describe the process steps that should be followed in order to meet a particular end.

Quality Standards for Specific Reporting Data: Describe the levels of data quality that must be met for a dataset to be considered of high enough quality for a specific use.

Statistical Agents: Organizations designated by the states that aggregate data from numerous companies for state regulators.

Review Questions

1. Establishing data standards formally defines expectations for the different characteristics of data: content, technical format, processes, and methodologies to prepare data or assess quality and actual quality levels required to meet requirements.

2. Insurance is a highly regulated industry that depends on the successful transfer of different kinds of information. Standards facilitate data transfer by providing guidance and a level of specifications for requirements from industry advisory boards, state regulators, the federal government, and international requirements for insurers who do business in multiple countries.

3. Insurers collect and assess data from individual customers and corporations, brokers, vendors, and health care providers. They share information within the organization to underwrite, issue, and administer policies, pay claims, develop products, and manage markets. They share information with regulators.

4. Standards make information provided by different carriers more consistent so data can be exchanged for reporting, analytics, rate setting, and ensuring market fairness.

5. Per ACORD, standards support the insurance industry in a number of ways:
   - For the wide variation in users of insurance data who have varying functional and technical demands, as well as goals and objectives, standards ensure that their varying needs can be met at a reasonable cost.
   - To address the exponential growth of relevant data, standards reduce the effects of variation for organizations keeping up with the increase in volume and velocity.
   - Standards enable insurance companies to better navigate macroeconomic, technical, and demographic changes, such as increasing consumer demands, an aging workforce, a complex regulatory environment, and technological obsolescence.

6. Focus areas for state regulation include:
   - **Insurer solvency**: In order to monitor the financial health of insurers to detect the potential for insolvency, insurers are required to report standard financial data to state regulators.
   - **Rates and products**: To balance the needs of insurers and consumers, rates must be adequate but not excessive, based on sound actuarial practice and not unfairly discriminatory. To demonstrate they meet these requirements, insurers collect and report specific types of data to state regulators, who determine appropriate rate levels and the adequacy of coverage for markets.
   - **Market structure and performance**: To support the availability and affordability of insurance, regulation focuses on ways to ensure coverage through pooling and reinsurance in situations where it would not be financially possible for an insurance company to provide it.
   - **Market conduct**: Focuses on risks associated with unfair trade practices to ensure insurers deal with applicants, insureds, claimants, and others fairly. Regulators rely on consumer complaints and other data.

7. Compliance with state regulations is complicated by the number of states, each with different regulations and a necessary level of detail. US and international regulations play a role in complicating compliance.

8. Organizations that help mitigate the effects of regulatory compliance include:
   - The National Association of Insurance Commissioners develops standards applicable across jurisdictions.
   - ACORD develops standards to facilitate the exchange of data.
   - IAIABC and WCIO develop and maintain standards related to workers' compensation.
   - WEDI develops standards related to the exchange and interoperability of health care data.

9. False: The insurance industry is also subject to federal and state regulation that focuses on concerns that include insurance, such as individual rights, consumer privacy, data sharing, and financial controls.

10. Insurers are subjected to the following federal, state, and international regulations:
    - Health Care Insurance Portability and Accountability Act (HIPAA).
    - Gramm-Leach-Bliley Act of 1999 (GLBA).

- U.S. PATRIOT Act.
- Sarbanes-OXLEY Act of 2002 (SOX).
- General Data Protection Regulation (GDPR).
- California Consumer Privacy Act (CCPA).

11. HIPAA is intended to modernize how health care information is collected, stored shared and protected. It limits the ability of insurers and providers to share information with a level of consent from patients and requires national standards for electronic health care transactions.

12. The five rules of HIPAA's Title II related to administrative simplification are:
    - The Privacy Rule describes national regulations for the use and disclosure of Protected Health Information (PHI) in healthcare treatment, payment, and operations. This provides the conditions under which PHI can be disclosed and those under which disclosure requires the data subjects' consent. It gives individuals the right to correct inaccurate information about themselves.
    - The Transactions and Code Sets Rule supports the intention of HIPAA to standardize the ways that health care plans engage in health care transactions, thus reducing complexity in the health care system.
    - The Security Rule supports the Privacy Rule in the context of electronic/digitally stored PHI. It requires that organizations that hold PHI must have administrative, physical safeguards to control access to PHI, and technical safeguards to ensure PHI is not intercepted in transmission.
    - The Unique Identifiers Rule required the creation of a new data element to support HIPAA: the National Provider Identifier (NPI). The NPI provides the basis for integrating records related to the same provider.
    - The Enforcement Rule stipulates the procedures for investigating potential HIPAA violations, such as the misuse of PHI, the failure to protect PHI, and the inability to provide patients access to PHI.

13. GLBA focused on the relationship between large financial institutions, including insurance companies, and the degree to which multiple kinds of activities (banking and insurance) could be carried on by the same organization.

14. Financial institutions are required to:
    - Have policies in place to protect information from foreseeable threats to security and data integrity.
    - Have a written information security plan that indicates by whom safeguards will be managed, how the information security plan will be managed, and how it will be adapted to changing practices in information collection, storage, and use.
    - Provide consumers with privacy notices describing what information is being collected about them, how that information would be used, with whom it would be shared, and how it would be protected; as well as how consumers could opt out of certain conditions.

15. The act allows increased data collection and sharing of personally identifiable information (PII) among government agencies, police, and financial institutions for the purpose of identifying and reporting activities that may involve money laundering or terrorist activities.

16. The ability to detect fraud, unexpected behavior, depends on having a clear picture of what expected behavior looks like. This picture is derived from the ability to detect meaningful patterns in data and to identify anomalies in the patterns.

17. SOX sets requirements for financial recordkeeping and reporting for publicly held corporations in the US, including a requirement that the leaders of corporations certify the accuracy of corporate

financial statements, thus making the board of directors accountable for the quality of organizational data. SOX has a direct result on how corporations validate and present information. It requires changes to corporate governance, internal controls, and financial disclosures. In order to attest to the accuracy of data, leadership must have a definition of accuracy and measurements of accuracy. SOX also requires evidence to show that data have been handled properly and that its integrity has been maintained from the point of origin to its use in financial reports.

18. The order addressed:
    - The risks of AI systems to national security.
    - The need to develop standards around trustworthiness.
    - The risks of developing biological materials and enabling fraud.
    - Concerns about privacy and called for federal agencies to evaluate the effectiveness of "privacy preserving techniques".
    - The risk to equity and civil rights, including algorithmic discrimination.
    - The need for advocacy for positive uses of AI in health care, education, government, and for consumers, and for its potential for innovation and competition.
    - The need for balance in support of workers and fair labor practices.

19. GDPR governs the use of personal data inside the EU, as well as the transfer of personal data outside the EU.
    - Gives individuals more control over their personal data.
    - Prevents the processing of data without a legal reason: consent from the data subject, contractual obligation, legal obligation, protection of vital interests of an individual, to perform tasks in the public interest, and to protect the interests of the data controller, provided these are not overridden by the interests of the data subject.
    - Clarifies the rights of the individual data subject with respect to data about them. Data collectors must be transparent about the data they have. People have the right to access their personal information, to know how it is being processed, and to have it removed or erased from the records of the data controller.

20. The regulatory standards require high-quality data and the ability to prove that the data is well managed. These regulations are based on the assumptions that data and metadata are reliable, personal data is protected, and the data is consistent and can be integrated and understood holistically.

21. Standards adopted by Insurance Services Office (ISO) and the National Council on Compensation Insurance (NCCI) to improve the consistency and quality of data include:
    - Adhere to standard codes for rating (Don't make codes up).
    - Use standard codes across jurisdiction (Don't make up different codes for different places).
    - Define conditions under which zeros and blanks have meaning and use these consistently.
    - Don't reuse old codes to represent new values.
    - Use only common abbreviations.
    - Use fields for one data element only (do not overload fields with multiple meanings).
    - Avoid creating redundant data elements – data elements should be mutually exclusive; they should not contain the same or overlapping concepts.

22. False. Technical standards allow an organization to use external data with limited data preparation work.

23. The technical requirements describe what content is required (data elements) and how content should be prepared and formatted (character sets, file formats) so that both can be transmitted,

received, and made usable. These standards also include requirements to ensure that data is compatible with the systems used by multiple stakeholders.

24. It is intended to provide guidance for actuaries (and others) in selecting data, assessing whether it is appropriate (relevant), reasonable, and comprehensive (containing all the data elements they need for their analysis) enough to be fit for purpose in their work products, and then making appropriate disclosures about any findings when they create their work products.

25. The Actuarial Standard of Practice No. 23 focuses on process by describing how to assess data sources and potential biases due to data issues, as well as how to report on corrections and adjustments made to data, and the degree to which an analysis depends on data supplied by others.

26. These may also include the methodology for measuring the quality of data or may describe how data should be prepared and evaluated so that it can be gathered and analyzed consistently.

27. NAIC's Statistical Handbook describes the methodology for assessing data quality as part of statistical reporting, providing a case study in applying data quality requirements within a data-centric process. It also demonstrates the value of understanding those requirements as part of a data supply chain.

28. Financial data provides quarterly and annual snapshots of an insurer's financial position, to be used to understand both short- and long-term financial performance. Financial data provides a way to evaluate solvency. Statistical data provides a way to understand the relationship between rates or between premiums and losses.

29. Statistical plans serve as de facto standards for the submission of data to the state regulators, via the statistical agents. Statistical agents maintain these plans, modifying them to ensure they conform to regulatory reporting requirements. Statistical plans define the data elements, formats, and time frames for company reporting, and instruct insurers how to code and submit their premium and loss data to the statistical agent.

30. False. Requirements are delineated for both the individual insurers who provide data to the statistical agents and for the statistical agents who provide it to the state.

31. The dimensions of quality and core data management practices addressed in the NAIC Handbook include:
    - **Accuracy:** Coding must be accurate based on what is known about the transaction. Details may be missing but should not contain incorrect or deceptive details.
    - **Data Quality Monitoring and Root Cause Analysis:** Data should be evaluated; the causes of systematic errors should be addressed, and data should be monitored to ensure that systematic errors do not reemerge.
    - **Completeness:** Control totals should be provided, and data should be reconciled to the Annual Statement.
    - **Validity:** Values should be within the domain of acceptable values.
    - **Reasonableness:** Checks that data is within reasonable or expected patterns, subject to business conditions.

32. The relationship between insurers, statistical agents, and state insurance commissioners can be understood through the concept of a supply chain, where each link represents a supplier/customer relationship.

Core Data Quality Management Functions

Educational Objectives

Upon completion of this assignment, you should be able to:

1. Understand each phase of the DQ Improvement Cycle in depth and explain how these can be applied to prevent errors and better manage data.
2. Describe how dimensions of quality can be used to develop standards that align with the expectations of internal and external stakeholders (e.g., those along the internal supply chain, as well as regulators, insurance commissioners, and industry associations).
3. Explain how data can be assessed for quality and how findings from assessments can be used to develop controls and monitoring routines that can raise organizational awareness of data quality levels and issues.
4. Explain what a data quality issue is and how data quality issues can be managed.
5. Describe the ways that data quality management can lead to process improvements throughout the organization.

For each assignment, define or describe each of the Key Terms and Concepts and answer each of the Review and Discussion Questions.

Key Terms and Concepts

Standards:

Data Profiling:

Data Assessment:

Data Profiling:

Preparation:

Analysis:

Assessment:

Action:

Controls:

Edits:

System and Processing Controls:

Threshold:

Data Issue:

Remediation:

Review Questions

1. What are the goals of the improvement cycle?

2. When should standards be applied and what effect do they have on data quality?

3. Identify things that can get in the way of enforcing data standards.

4. How does data profiling use dimensions to understand the quality of column data?

5. What insights can be derived from data profiling at the record level?

6. What insights can be derived from data profiling at the dataset level?

7. Where do the requirements for standards and measurements of data quality come from? How are they implemented?

8. Describe how to define a field standard for completeness.

9. What monitoring rule can be implemented for field completeness?

10. What is a question that should be asked when developing a field standard for format correctness? How can the rules be defined based on the answer to the questions?

11. Describe how the field standard for validity can be defined and what a monitoring rule would look like.

12. The text provides a template for defining a standard. What kinds of information can be included?

13. Which of the following statements is true?

    A. Requirements can be derived from the perspective of a process that is supplying data downstream or from that of a processing consuming upstream data. There is no advantage to reviewing from both sides.
    B. Data standards provide the basis for the assessment of data, but can also be formulated based on findings from assessments.
    C. Data assessment is a separate activity from determining the implications of the findings.
    D. All of the above are true.

14. How do analysts use data profiling and what value does it bring to data quality efforts?

15. Which of the following statements is true of an initial instance of data profiling?

    A. Initial data profiling focuses on discovering the rules and relationships of the data in a column.
    B. Initial data profiling should focus not only on the data but also on the metadata to clarify any misconceptions about the data.
    C. The input to profiling is accurate data and metadata.
    D. All of the above are true.

16. Which of the following is true of the preparation phase of an initial data profiling assessment?

    A. Preparation includes researching and reviewing documentation that describes how the data to be assessed is created, maintained, stored, shared, and used, as well as any metadata.
    B. Preparation includes understanding the purpose of the assessment, which will determine the scope and depth of the analysis.
    C. Research involves working with subject matter experts who can share information about known data issues or business processes/systems that support the production of the data.
    D. All of the above are true.

17. In addition to column-level statistics, the initial analysis of data profiling should include what other analyses?

18. What types of information can be derived from column-level statistics?

19. All of the following statements are true of column-level statistics in the assessment phase of data profiling except:

A. Cardinality counts help identify the key structure of the file, enable high-level reasonability checks, and identify fields with duplicative or related information.
B. The count and percentage of null or blank values help identify missing data and fields with related data.
C. Statistics on null values are critical because nulls represent data issues.
D. The percentage unique statistic is another way of looking at cardinality.

20. All of the following statements are true of column-level statistics in the assessment phase of data profiling except:

A. Minimum and maximum values help identify outliers, which may be data issues.
B. Format patterns analysis represents a challenge since for many fields the pattern isn't relevant to identifying data problems, e.g., first name.
C. Data pattern analysis can be problematic if the data is associated with multiple data types.
D. Frequency distributions are an effective tool, even when the cardinality of the field is high.

21. What processes are involved in the data quality assessment?

22. What data quality issues can data quality assessment help identify?

23. Output from the data quality assessment process should include what pieces of information? What value do these provide?

24. How do action items differ based on the goal of data profiling?

25. Why are controls more focused than baseline assessment of data and what purpose do they serve?

26. For each of the types of data quality controls, identify issues that might make them challenging to apply.

27. Other than detecting errors, how can data monitoring support data quality?

28. Why are tolerances important? What kinds of interventions might be applied based on tolerance?

29. Data quality reporting:

    A. Raises awareness and develops understanding of improvement processes.
    B. Should be designed to enable intervention in the technical process and provide that information in a meaningful way.
    C. Has multiple audiences who receive the same report at different times.
    D. Should be tied to divisional goals and the critical data needs of that division.

30. Identify and describe the phases of data quality management.

31. Which of the following statements is true about data issues?

    A. Data issues are generally found through the failure of technical processes.
    B. Who identifies the data issue is the most important detail to record and track for remediation purposes.
    C. What is identified as a data issue may be a symptom of a different issue.
    D. All of the above are true.

32. Issue management uses an iterative process to define the real problem with data. What questions should be asked?

33. Although quantifying the size and scope of an issue is important to defining it, what considerations will impact the decision whether and how to remediate an issue?

34. Based on the relative importance of the issues and the results of cost-benefit analyses, issue remediation will be prioritized. How might the priority of issues determine remediation?

35. How do data quality management activities improve existing business and technical processes throughout the organization?

36. How does process improvement lead to improvement in data quality?

37. List the improvement opportunities presented by process improvement.

38. How can knowledge gained from the entire improvement cycle be used to improve an organization's business data and processes?

39. True or False: As an organization evolves by adding new customers, developing new products, and adopting new technologies, the data quality improvement cycle provides a means of responding to change, ensuring data is reliable and usable.

Discussion Questions

NOTE: The questions below are intended to continue to challenge you to test your knowledge of the required reading by applying what you have studied to real-life situations.

No suggested answers are provided at the end of the assignment for these types of open discussion questions. Answers may vary by student and will depend on their organization's culture, resources, and processes.

1. Discuss your company's approach to data quality management. What role or roles do you play?

2. What types of reporting do you use or create? Who is your audience and what information do they need?

3. If you are a consumer of data quality reporting, how complete is the information you receive? If you were in charge, what changes would you make?

Answers to Assignment 7 Questions

NOTE: These answers are provided to give students a basic understanding of acceptable types of responses. They are often not the only valid answers and are not intended to provide an exhaustive response to the questions.

Key Terms and Concepts

Standards: Describe what high-quality data means by setting or implying expectations for the condition of data in any given instance.

Data Profiling: An analysis technique that produces frequency distributions at the column level.

Data Assessment: The process of observing characteristics of data to identify differences between expectations for data (e.g., standards, rules, etc.) and the condition of the actual data.

Data Profiling: A specific form of data analysis that uses high-level statistics (cardinality, percentage of NULL values, MIN/MAX values, format, and key structure analysis) along with frequency distribution to enable inferences about the quality of data.

Preparation: Baseline assessment phase, defining goals and scope, and gathering information that will support analysis.

Analysis: Baseline assessment phase, making observations about the data in order to understand its quality.

Assessment: Baseline assessment phase synthesizing observations in order to understand their implications.

Action: Baseline assessment phase, creating and executing a plan to address findings from the assessment and to propose improvements that result in more reliable data.

Controls: An automated or manual means of providing feedback within a system or process.

Edits: Data quality controls that prevent data collection or input issues on the front end.

System and Processing Controls: Ensure data retains its integrity as it is moved along the data supply chain and processed.

Threshold: An indicator of how much error (or change) is allowable by a process before the results of the process are of such low quality that the process can be said to have failed.

Data Issue: Any obstacle to the use of data, regardless of how it is caused or how it might be remediated. Issues may be simple or complex, ranging from questions about data definition and permitted use to addressing unexpected changes in financial trends that require analysis of multiple inputs.

Remediation: The process of making changes to business and technical processes and/or the data itself, in order to remove the issue.

Review Questions

1. Goals of the improvement cycle include:
   - Clarify expectations for data so that these expectations can be met.
   - Understand the processes that create data and improve them to produce higher-quality data.
   - Increase awareness and knowledge about data so that data creators and custodians can help ensure organizational data is fit for the purposes of data consumers.

2. Data standards should be applied when expectations for the condition of the data are understood and can be enforced. When this happens, they result in more complete, accurate, and consistent data.

3. Things that can get in the way of enforcing data standards include:

   - **Cost**: Building and implementing technical and process controls takes time and effort.
   - **Ambiguity**.
     - Standards require interpretation; skills to formulate the rules that accurately represent the requirements of the standards.
     - There may be a number of requirements and standards, so enforcement may require knowledge of those multiple sets of rules.
     - Different uses may require different standards.
   - **Lack of options for enforcement**: not every standard can be enforced through a rule, especially at the dataset level.
   - **Customization**: For insurance products in particular, the level of customization can make standards impossible to define.
   - **Volatility**: As the business and regulatory environments evolve, standards must evolve as well. Documentation is key to sharing and managing them.

4. Data profiling provides insight into the overall population of the column by identifying the completeness (% Null or default), the consistency of data types, and the validity of individual values.

5. Records can be understood as:
   - Complete or incomplete based on the population of a subset of fields.
   - Current or out-of-date based on the processes through which they are maintained.
   - To have or lack integrity based on their connections to other records.

6. Datasets may be understood as:
   - Complete or incomplete by reconciliation to data in a source system or comparisons of past instances of the dataset itself.
   - Current or out-of-date, depending on whether they contain all records created within a given timeframe.
   - To have or lack integrity based on whether they have or do not have the expected relationship with other datasets.

7. Standards and data quality measurements are derived from the requirements of internal processes, from consumers along the data chain, and from external stakeholders. Standards can be implemented as front-end controls to prevent records from being created when quality standards are not met. They can also be used to develop data monitoring routines for processes or systems.

8. If the field is mandatory, a front-end control can prevent the record from being created unless the field is populated. If the field is not mandatory but other fields on the record help determine whether the field must be populated, a control can be developed based on the other fields.

9. A completeness data quality monitoring rule can measure the ratio of records with a valid value to the total number of records, expressed as a percentage.

10. Does the field have a unique (one-and-only one) format or can it have multiple formats? If the field has a unique format, then the rule is simple. However, care should be taken that everyone agrees on the format. If the field has multiple formats and there is a benefit to measuring the format, then each acceptable and unacceptable format must be identified.

11. If there is a defined domain of valid values, then a control can test for allowable values. A monitoring rule would measure the percentage of records where a valid code is reported against the total number of records in the dataset where the field is expected to be populated.

    If the domain of valid values is not static, then the control and measuring rule must be kept up-to-date. Also, it may be important to maintain information on which values were valid at different points in time.

    If there is no defined domain of values, an edit may be put in place to prevent the creation of records with clearly invalid values in the field. A monitoring rule would need to be measured by looking at records with invalid values or outliers.

    If there are relationships between fields, a control could prevent records with invalid relationships from being created. A monitoring rule would measure the percentage of records with the valid combinations against the total records where the field is expected to be populated.

12. A template for defining a standard can include:
    - Field name.
    - Physical field name.
    - Definition.
    - Uses.
    - General quality.
    - Completeness rule.
    - Format rule.
    - Validity rule.
    - Use of default values.
    - Front-end control.
    - Data quality measurement.

13. B. Looking at both sides can help identify data gaps or differences that may be obstacles to use. Assessment should also describe the analyst's conclusions and/or hypotheses about the impact of the findings, including the sharing of those findings with stakeholders.

14. Using data proofing statistics, analysts can understand characteristics of data structure and relationships within a dataset, as well as column-level details for relatively large datasets. These details can be very valuable in data development efforts, data migrations, and in determining whether data is fit for a specific purpose.

15. B. Profiling can be applied to columns or datasets. Input to profiling includes accurate and inaccurate data and metadata.

16. D.

17. In addition to column-level statistics, the initial analysis of data profiling should include:
    - Understand the business process that generates the data as a source of expectations for data.
    - Identify risks associated with the originating business processes, as well as those associated with data movement and transformation.
    - Assess the completeness and integrity of the data model, as well as the quality and sufficiency of metadata and reference data.

18. Information that can be derived from column-level statistics includes:
    - Cardinality count representing the number of distinct values in a column.
    - Percentage unique represented by the ratio of the number of distinct values to the number of rows.
    - Percentage and count NULL represents the portion of records that have no values populated.
    - Percentage and count Blank represents the portion of records where blank or space is populated.
    - Minimum and maximum values representing the lowest and highest values reported.
    - Format and data type pattern describes the range of formats presented in a given column.
    - Frequency distributions provide the count and percentage calculation for each value in a column.

19. C. Null values are not necessarily data problems.

20. D. Frequency distributions can be difficult to use when the cardinality is high.

21. Data quality assessment is the process of observing data characteristics via inspection and analysis in order to draw conclusions about the quality of the data. This process should include a comparison of an instance of data to the rules, standards, and other characteristics that define its quality. Data quality assessment can be the means of defining or clarifying rules and expectations when they are not known.

22. Data quality assessment can help identify data issues, at-risk data, and risks associated with the use of the data. As the organization matures, assessment can be done from both directions, through knowledge of existing rules and standards, and as a means to learn about new or unfamiliar datasets.

23. Output from the assessment process should include objective descriptions of the condition of data compared to expectations and documentation of the relation of the data's condition to processes and systems. Outputs provide the basis for developing action items to improve the data and metadata. Output is also the basis for developing and implementing controls to prevent data issues and rules to monitor data quality.

24. If a goal of data profiling is to identify data issues, then action items will involve reporting findings to the owners of the source systems to correct records, implement controls, or improve business and technical processes. If profiling is done to support the development of a new system or application, then action items will focus on informing the project team of any findings that might influence the data model or the design and orchestration of the system.
    If profiling is done to establish monitoring rules, then action items will include confirming which data is most valuable to monitor and refining monitoring rules so that they provide useful feedback about data quality conditions.

25. Controls are directed at data that has the most importance to the business and is at risk of being incorrect or missing without proper controls. Controls:
    - Prevent data collection or input issues on the front-end edits.
    - Ensure data retains its integrity as it is moved along the supply chain and is processed, including balancing record counts, monitoring batch jobs, and system-to-system financial reconciliation.
    - Monitor the quality of data by measuring data against defined rules, historical patterns, or other standards to mitigate risk.

26. Prevention on the front end should be applied whenever possible to prevent any errors through front-end edits. However, the rules for these edits are costly to implement and maintain. Decisions on which edits to implement should be made based on how critical the data is in its originating process and its use downstream. System and process controls are intended to ensure the integrity of data as it moves through the data supply chain. Controls on data movement depend on the type of data being moved, the technology used to move and store it, and the risks being mitigated through the controls. Monitoring the profile of data is more complex. Depending on data content, data "shape" can be defined by the distribution of values in particular columns, the distribution of financial data over time, or other data characteristics. Monitoring works on data characteristics or relationships that are expected to have a degree of similarity over time.

27. In addition to identifying errors, monitoring can be used to detect changes in the level of error in a dataset over time, as a form of trend analysis. It can also detect unexpected changes in product mix, distribution of customers across markets or financial data across other variables.

28. Tolerances provide a basis for making different kinds of interventions depending on the degree of error in a dataset of process. If no errors or significant changes are detected, then data processing completes, and data consumers are informed that it has been successful. If errors or changes detected are within tolerances, then data processing completes, and data consumers are informed that the data contains errors and that these errors are within tolerance. If errors or changes detected exceed tolerances, then data processing may be stopped, or it may be paused so that errors can be investigated.

29. B.

30. The phases of the data quality management include:
    - **Identification and definition**: Finding issues and providing initial definitions in preparation for analysis.
    - **Analysis and quantification**: Understanding the size and scope of data impacted by the issue and business processes affected by the issue, as well as determining the issue's root causes.
    - **Prioritization**: Assessing the business implications of the issue and defining the costs and benefits of remediation, in order to determine the relative importance of the issue.
    - **Remediation**: Dependent on the priority, complexity, and root causes of an issue, the process of making changes to business and technical processes and/or the data itself, in order to remove the issue.

31. C. There are a number of ways to find data issues. It is important to determine when, where and how, in addition to who.

32. Questions that should be asked to define the real problem with data include:
    - **Size/Scope**: Is the issue associated with one source system or multiple source systems?
    - **Data Impact**: How big is the issue in terms of the data? How many records are affected?

- **Timeframe:** Is the issue isolated to a single date or other timeframe? Has the problem changed over time?
- **Related Data:** Are the impacted data elements related to other data elements within the dataset?
- **Business Impact:** How many customers or clients are associated with the impacted data? Is the problem isolated to a few accounts or many?

33. The decision is based on the cost of remediation and the quantification of the issue's business impact, including understanding the uses of the data, the importance of those uses to the business strategy, the implications of having incorrect or incomplete data, and the cost and complexity of the remediation process.

34. Low-priority issues may not be remediated at all. High-priority issues may require both short-term (tactical) and long-term (strategic/root cause) remediation. Complex issues often have complex root causes and may require changes to both business and technical processes and the relationship between them.

35. The data quality activities of assessment, monitoring, and analysis, including root cause analysis, help an organization understand its existing business and technical processes, showing limitations and complexities. From this knowledge, it can eliminate, streamline, and improve existing processes.

36. Process improvement begins with an understanding of the organization's view of itself, its organizational data, and its business operations. When data quality issues identify something isn't working in the current state, i.e., data issues, root cause analysis of the data issues amounts to root cause analysis of business problems and inefficiencies. Remediation must address data and the processes.

37. Improvement opportunities presented by process improvement include:
    - Clarification of goals and requirements.
    - Simplification of business and technical processes.
    - Implementation of preventive controls.
    - Improvements in metadata and metadata management.
    - Training opportunities.

38. Knowledge from the improvement cycle can be used to implement business and technical process improvements, prevent data issues, enforce standards, and increase the overall trustworthiness of data.

39. True.

Data Quality Tools

Educational Objectives

Upon completion of this assignment, you should be able to:

1. Explain the different categories of tools that can influence the quality of data.
2. Explain the functionality of tools that support core data quality management processes (data profiling and assessment, monitoring, issue management, and reporting).
3. Describe the ways that tools designed to support other aspects of data management - metadata management, data architecture, reference and master data management, ETL (extract, transform, load), and data ingestion - contribute to data quality management.
4. Explain the process of choosing tools to support data quality management, including factors that should be accounted for to ensure long-term value from tools.

For each assignment, define or describe each of the Key Terms and Concepts and answer each of the Review and Discussion Questions.

Key Terms and Concepts

Rules Library:

Exception Records:

Data Query Tools:

Data Visualization Tools:

Lineage:

Track and Trace Analysis:

File Checks on Data Received:

Balance Controls:

Process Timing Controls:

Architectural Tools:

Architectural Flow Diagram:

Data Modeling Tools:

Business Glossary:

Data Catalog:

Data Cataloging Tools:

Data Dictionaries:

Business Rules Engines:

Master Data:

Reference Data:

Data Preparation and Processing Tools:

Review Questions

1. What is the purpose of tooling?

2. Choosing a tool is not a straightforward process. What are some of the issues that should be considered when evaluating tools?

3. How does tooling help support implementing and maintaining data standards?

4. True or False: Defining requirements and adopting standards is a human-intensive activity.

5. Identify some of the functionality of data profiling tools.

6. One root cause analysis technique is the "Five Whys". What is the technique and how does it help root cause analysis?

7. How can track and trace as a root cause analysis be facilitated?

8. Which of the following is true?

    A. Query tools help analysts understand the context of errors.
    B. Visualization tools help detect patterns that may be difficult to see in rows of data.
    C. Lineage and metadata tools help trace the route data takes as it moves through the organization and the effects of inputs or specific process steps on data with identified issues.
    D. All of the above are true.

9. Which of the following is not true?

    A. Tools can answer the question "Why?"
    B. Tools can pinpoint coding errors and gaps in logic.
    C. Tools can provide information to help confirm or rule out hypotheses about root causes.
    D. All of the above are not true.

10. True or False: Data problems isolated in one system have the same priority as one that causes issues in multiple downstream systems.

11. Which of the following is true?

    A. The sole purpose of controls is to prevent data issues.
    B. Front-end controls prevent bad data from being created; thus, they are data quality tools.
    C. Data profiling tools are data quality tools.
    D. All of the above are true.

12. Where are upfront controls established, what are they based on, and how can they support process development?

13. Why are automated data quality tools preferred over manual?

14. True or False: Data quality monitoring tools should include file checks on data received, balance controls, and process timing controls.

15. What is the most effective way to use technical process controls and the analytics that result?

16. True or False: Data reporting tools are separate from data quality profiling and monitoring tools.

17. What basic functionality is required for reporting on results?

18. What are the two steps in developing reports and what are the considerations for each?

19. What functionality must an issue management tool have?

20. What is the purpose of architectural tools in terms of data quality?

21. Identify different types of metadata critical to data governance.

22. What are the goals of a business glossary?

23. In what ways is a business glossary central to both data governance and data stewardship?

24. Data cataloging functionality should:

25. Which of the following statements is true?

    A. Data dictionaries may contain information such as key structures for tables to make it easier for data consumers to use data.
    B. Data dictionaries are such a key source of metadata that they are well-managed.
    C. There is no reason to integrate data dictionaries, data catalogs, and business glossaries.
    D. All of the above are true.

26. True or False: Without clear processes for creating and maintaining data dictionaries, they may only exist embedded in data models, specifications, or spreadsheets.

27. What purposes do business rules serve?

28. What are the questions data lineage asks, and why is it valuable?

29. What questions are important to ask before developing a lineage tool or selecting one from the market?

30. Identify the requirements for tools for master data and reference data.

31. What functionality can data processing tools include to make data fit for purpose?

32. What ways can data processing tools be used to enhance data?

33. What should the data quality team consider when evaluating a data quality tool?

34. True or False: The first step in evaluating data quality tools is to talk to the various vendors of tools to determine the functionality of their products.

35. What are some ways to define the data quality problems that need to be solved? What activities help develop requirements for data quality tools before evaluating any tools?

36. Describe the process that should be used to evaluate tools.

37. Identify factors that will lead to the successful selection and integration of data quality tools.

Discussion Questions

NOTE: The questions below are intended to continue to challenge you to test your knowledge of the required reading by applying what you have studied to real-life situations.

No suggested answers are provided at the end of the assignment for these types of open discussion questions. Answers may vary by student and will depend on their organization's culture, resources, and processes.

1. What data quality tools are in use in your organization?

2. What process was used to evaluate and select tools? What were the strengths of the process? The weaknesses?

3. How successful has the use of these tools been? What problems have been experienced?

Answers to Assignment 8 Questions

NOTE: These answers are provided to give students a basic understanding of acceptable types of responses. They are often not the only valid answers and are not intended to provide an exhaustive response to the questions.

Key Terms and Concepts

Rules Library: Used to build, store, and maintain technical versions of DQ standards.

Exception Records: Data that breaks defined rules or that includes characteristics that analysts will want to see more detail about.

Data Query Tools: Tools that allow analysts to delve further into relationships and rules.

Data Visualization Tools: Tools that allow analysts to see a wider dataset in a condensed visual form, especially if profiling statistics are supplemented with additional information gathered from querying data.

Lineage: A form of metadata that describes the movement of data along the internal data supply chain, from origin in a source system through its uses in downstream processes.

Track and Trace Analysis: In situations where the root cause is not associated with the system in which the data was assessed, trace the data back through the internal data supply chain to identify where the issue is first detectable.

File Checks on Data Received: Controls that confirm that all required data objects have been received for a batch process and that they are in condition to be processed.

Balance Controls: Controls that measure the completeness of data as it moves from source to target.

Process Timing Controls: Controls that focus on the timing and duration of data processing jobs in order to detect jobs that run unexpectedly short or long or that fail.

Architectural Tools: Provide a picture of the data landscape at different levels of abstraction.

Architectural Flow Diagram: An architectural tool that provides a basic form of application-to-application data lineage.

Data Modeling Tools: An architectural tool that represents data at the object and attribute level.

Business Glossary: A system used to document and manage terms and definitions needed to understand an organization's business concepts and to describe the relationships among concepts.

Data Catalog: An inventory of data within an organization.

Data Cataloging Tools: Manage enterprise data platforms and provide a means of cataloging data at the enterprise level by scanning the environment to collect fundamental technical metadata about data objects and their attributes, including physical names, data types, formats, and definitions.

Data Dictionaries: Describes the objects and data elements for a specific system or application (i.e., for relational data, this means definitions of tables and columns).

Business Rules Engines: A defined constraint on a business process.

Master Data: Represents core business objects, the things that matter most to the organization.

Reference Data: Consists of codified data values and their meanings, also known as look-up data.

Data Preparation and Processing Tools: Include those that execute traditional ETL (extract, transform, load), as well as those that extract, load (or ingest), and then transform.

Review Questions

1. Tooling:
   - Enables data quality processes.
   - Can automate aspects of data management processes.
   - Can support data quality management processes with workflows.
   - Can support data quality management by storing data and metadata for reference, reporting, and analytics.

2. When evaluating tools, consider the following:
   - Data quality tools do not do the same things in the same way. Beware of the shiny object response.
   - Choices in tools should be grounded in the problems the organization is trying to solve. How will the tools be used? Who will review the output? What actions are expected to be taken based on it?
   - Evaluating tools and planning for their use should include an understanding of the data quality management practices and of an approach to business process and technical development that starts with high-quality, trustworthy data in mind.

3. Tooling helps support implementing and maintaining data standards in the following ways:
   - Tools ensure that once standards are defined and clarified, they are documented in consistent ways and stored so as to be easily accessible and maintained.
   - Tools enable rules to be translated into technical rules so they can be executed consistently.
   - Some tools make rules available to technical processes.

4. True.

5. Data profiling tool should:
   - Enable the discovery of data structure, including the probable relationships between data objects (files and tables).
   - Incorporate a rules library.
   - Support anomaly detection through more sophisticated statistics.
   - Enable review of exception records.

6. When investigating a data issue, ask the question "Why?" at least five times to drill into the symptoms of a problem. This helps separate the symptoms from the underlying causes of a problem.

7. Metadata that describes data movement and structure, including business process descriptions, architectural diagrams, mapping documents, lineage, and data processing code, facilitates tracking and tracing.

8. D.

9. A.

10. False. Data problems that cause issues in multiple downstream systems have a higher priority.

11. C.

12. Upfront controls are established as part of the application design process. They should be based on data quality standards and requirements. If these standards and requirements do not exist, the process of designing controls will provide the impetus to clarify what standards should be.

13. Manual tools, which are not scalable, only provide information, not control. Automated monitoring, executed as part of data processing, ensures that measurements are taken at a set frequency, rules are executed consistently, and results are stored in a way that enables trend analysis and other analytics. In addition to error counts, automated monitoring can provide statistical calculations that automate comparisons to previous results.

14. False. These functions are process controls, not data quality monitoring controls.

15. As with data quality monitoring controls, the results of technical process control measurements should be stored in a way that facilitates use in analytics. The analytics should also be automated so that anomalies can be flagged based on statistics.

16. False. Data profiling and monitoring tools provide results that can be given to stakeholders. There is no need for separate reporting tools.

17. Visualization, annotation, and the ability to drill down into the details of a given finding are necessary functionalities for reporting.

18. The first step is to understand the requirements: what risks are stakeholders trying to mitigate? What questions do they want answered? What level of detail will help them understand the answers to those questions? The second step is to translate those requirements into reports that can answer those questions. The consideration here is whether the functionality of profiling tools is adequate or whether data must be extracted from the profiling tools and read into a visualization tool.

19. An issue management tool must:
    - Provide an issue identifier by which the problem can be tracked.
    - Capture basic information about the issue.
    - Classify each issue along the lines important for reporting.
    - Connect related issues within the tool.
    - Record and classify the details about each issue.
    - Record the root causes of each issue.
    - Enable status reporting.

20. Architectural tools capture assumptions about what constitutes high-quality data in any given instance.

21. Metadata critical to data governance includes:
    - Business Glossary.
    - Data Catalog.
    - Data Dictionary.

- Business Rule Engine.
- Lineage Documentation.

22. The goals of a business glossary are:
    - Enable people to understand each other.
    - Drive toward a consistent identification of and consistent naming of data.
    - Supply system-agnostic information to support data use.

23. A business glossary is central to both data governance and data stewardship since it:
    - Enables the identification of categories and types of data that have particular governance requirements.
    - Enables the documentation of both a common vocabulary – business terms that represent agreed-to standards – and an uncommon vocabulary – business terms that have different meanings in different parts of the organization.

24. Data cataloging functionality should:
    - Connect to a wide range of different technical environments and formats to scan.
    - Allow for rescans of the same environments to identify and record changes to data structures.
    - Identify some critical data elements based on known characteristics of the values associated with those elements so they can be effectively protected.
    - Enable catalog metadata to be augmented by metadata from other sources.
    - Make metadata available to analysts and other data consumers.

25. A.

26. True.

27. Business rules describe what must happen or cannot happen within a process. They can be used as requirements for technical processes and to establish data quality expectations. When included in a data quality tool, they can be used for data cleansing and transformation.

28. By following data through processes and transformations, data lineage answers the questions of what person or process created the data, how the data has changed since it was originally created, and in which systems the change occurs. This helps analysts understand the kinds of changes that have been made to data along the data chain, providing insight into the root causes of data issues. Data lineage also supports impact analysis for systems development, change management, and data quality analysis. Finally, it enables understanding of where "the same data might exist in multiple systems.

29. Before developing a lineage tool or selecting one from the market, ask:
    - What level of lineage is required/desired?
    - How well will the tool work within the organization's technical environment?
    - How much maintenance will be required to ensure the ongoing accuracy of the output from the tool?
    - How is the tool likely to be used before making decisions about implementing it?

30. Requirements for tools for master data and reference data include:
    - For master data, the tool must be able to match and merge records accurately with minimal cases of false positives or false negatives.
    - For reference data, the tool must accommodate reference datasets of different levels of complexity and enable both manual and automated updates.

- The tool must work within the organization's technical environment to be able to send and receive data from other systems.

31. To make data fit for purpose, data processing tools should:
    - Enforce constraints.
    - Deduplicate data.
    - Perform validation.
    - Cleanse data.
    - Standardize data.

32. Ways that data processing tools can be used to enhance data include:
    - Integrating data from different sources together in the same table or file so it can be used as a single dataset.
    - Aggregating sets of records so that a new and different type of record is produced.
    - Augmenting or enriching a dataset by adding data so that the dataset can be used for additional purposes or with additional precision.

33. When evaluating a data quality tool, the data quality team should consider:
    - Defining the problems the organization is trying to solve.
    - Defining requirements, focusing on what the organization actually needs the tool to do rather than on the range of things the tool can do.
    - Understanding how the tools will work within the organization's technical environment, and what limitations or challenges the tool may present.
    - Preparing from a process perspective to use tools in ways that add value; envisioning how the tool improves a current process or supports a proposed process.

34. False. The first step is to assess the current state of data management practices in the organization and determine the biggest opportunities for improvement.

35. To define data quality problems that need to be solved, interview people about their concerns and pain points, and review documented pain points in the form of help desk tickets, incident reports, and audit findings. To help develop requirements for a data quality tool, develop scenarios for what the organization needs to accomplish, question all assumptions, and ask users to envision how a tool would fit in their process.

36. To evaluate tools:
    - Scan the market to determine what tools are available.
    - Consider what percentage of requirements the tool meets. Does it meet all requirements?
    - Ask organizations that use the tool what problems they are trying to solve, whether the tools helped solve the problem, and what limitations and challenges they experienced with the tool.
    - Evaluate the vendor: How long have they been in business? How many customers do they have?
    - What level of support does the vendor offer for initial installation and configuration, as well as ongoing support?
    - Consider budget, training requirements, and data management maturity.
    - Assess the compatibility of the tool's functionality and the organization's technical environment.
    - Ask users how a particular tool would be used, considering both automated and manual processes.

37. Factors that will lead to successful selection and integration of data quality tools include:
    - Problem statements to help the organization recognize improvement opportunities leading to requirements that are the basis for solutions to those problems.
    - Clear requirements that define the goals for the use of the tools and knowledge of what can be accomplished through specific forms of automation.
    - Reliable information about the technical environment, including the ability to identify and test risks related to technology.
    - Understanding the context of tool use and defining the processes that the tools are intended to support helps create a path to value by ensuring that:
        - Tools are supported by appropriate infrastructure.
        - Operational support is in place, including SLA (service level agreements), and support for upgrades to new versions of the tools.
        - End user support is in place, including basic help desk and "Ask an Expert" levels.
        - Teams using the tools are properly staffed.
        - End users have the training and ongoing support they need to execute their processes.
        - There is an escalation path for problems with the tools.
        - Benefits related to the processes the tools support are communicated to stakeholders.

Data Quality in the Context of Data Management

Educational Objectives

Upon completion of this assignment, you should be able to:

1. Understand and explain the purpose and benefits of data management frameworks.
2. Summarize the components of the DAMA (Data Management Association) DMBOK2 and EDM (Enterprise Data Management Council) DCAM and describe how these frameworks differ from each other.
3. Explain the ways different data management functional areas can influence the quality of organizational data.
4. Describe how the ISO 8000 Data Quality Management Process Reference Model presents an alternative way of looking at data quality management, as the core of data management, rather than a function within data management.
5. Understand and explain how adopting a framework can benefit an organization.
6. Explain factors that should be taken into consideration when adopting a framework.

For each assignment, define or describe each of the Key Terms and Concepts and answer each of the Review and Discussion Questions.

Key Terms and Concepts

Functional Areas:

Data Architecture:

Data Modeling and Design:

Data Warehousing and Business Intelligence:

Data Integration and Interoperability or Data in Motion:

Data Storage and Operations:

Reference and Master Data Management (MDM):

Document and Content Management:

Data Security:

Metadata Management:

Data Quality Management:

Data Governance:

DCAM2 Foundational Activities:

DCAM2 Execution Capabilities:

DCAM2 Collaboration Capability:

DCAM2 Application Capability:

Review Questions

1. How does a framework support data management?

2. What is the purpose of the Data Management Body of Knowledge (DMBOK)?

3. Describe the components of the DAMA DMBOK2 Data Management Framework?

4. What doesn't the DAMA Wheel imply and what questions are raised by the DAMA Wheel?

5. How did DAMA attempt to resolve the questions raised by the DAMA Wheel and how does this address the questions?

6. How many functional areas are DAMA's DMBOK organized, and how are they categorized in relation to the data life cycle?

7. Identify how the functional areas of the DAMA DMBOK fit into the data life cycle as either a phase or foundational, i.e., connected to all phases of the life cycle.

8. Identify the ways that the DAMA functional areas influence the quality of an organization's data.

9. Describe the structure of the Data Management Capability Assessment Model (DCAM) second release (DCAM2).

10. What are the purposes of the foundation activities of the DCAM2?

11. How do the foundational activities of the DCAM2 model support data quality efforts?

12. What are the purposes of the execution capabilities of the DCAM2 model?

13. How do the execution capabilities support data quality efforts?

14. What activities are included in the Data Control Environment, the only capability of the DCAM2's collaboration circle?

15. True or False: The DMBOK control environment extends across the execution components of data management.

16. Why is the Application circle of the DCAM2 model and its analytics management capability significant for data quality?

17. How do the DMBOK2 and DCAM/DCAM2 models differ?

18. What are some of the challenges or limitations of both DAMA and EDM frameworks?

19. How is the ISO model useful in relation to data quality and data management functions?

20. How does the ISO model apply the Shewhart Cycle: Plan, Do, Check, Act?

21. True or False: All three frameworks, DMBOK, DCAM, and ISO, specifically address the need to have the people in place with the necessary skills, tools, and processes to get the work done.

22. What are some thoughts to keep in mind when considering a framework?

23. True or False: The goal of data management is to implement a framework. High-quality data will follow.

24. What is the value in looking at different frameworks?

25. What is the biggest risk to adopting a framework? How does an organization limit the risk?

Discussion Questions

NOTE: The questions below are intended to continue to challenge you to test your knowledge of the required reading by applying what you have studied to real-life situations.

No suggested answers are provided at the end of the assignment for these types of open discussion questions. Answers may vary by student and will depend on their organization's culture, resources, and processes.

1. Does your organization have a framework it uses to implement data management? If so, can you identify it? How does the framework impact you and your work directly?

2. If there is a framework in place, how has it improved data quality? If there is no framework, how do you think the adoption of one might improve the data you work with?

3. How has culture changed to support the framework? If your organization hasn't adopted one, what changes to culture would you expect to see?

Answers to Assignment 9 Questions

NOTE: These answers are provided to give students a basic understanding of acceptable types of responses. They are often not the only valid answers and are not intended to provide an exhaustive response to the questions.

Key Terms and Concepts

Functional Areas: Per the DMBOK, represent the activities that contribute to an organization's ability to manage its data over time and in relation to phases of the data life cycle.

Data Architecture: Defines the blueprint for managing data assets by aligning with organizational strategy and establishing designs to meet strategic data requirements.

Data Modeling and Design: The process of discovering, analyzing, representing, and communicating data requirements in a precise form called the data model.

Data Warehousing and Business Intelligence: The planning, implementation, and control processes to manage decision support data and to enable data consumers to get value from data via analysis and reporting.

Data Integration and Interoperability or Data in Motion: Processes related to the movement and consolidation of data within and between data stores, applications, and organizations.

Data Storage and Operations: The work related to ongoing maintenance of stored data, to ensure that data itself is available and accessible, and that systems are performant so that the organization can use and get value from its data.

Reference and Master Data Management (MDM): Both include ongoing reconciliation and maintenance of core critical shared data to enable consistent use across systems of the most accurate, timely, and relevant version of truth about essential business entities.

Document and Content Management: Planning, implementation, and control activities to manage the lifecycle of data and information found in a range of unstructured media, especially documents needed to support legal and regulatory compliance requirements.

Data Security: Ensures that data privacy and confidentiality are maintained, that data is not breached, and that data is accessed appropriately.

Metadata Management: Planning, implementation, and control activities to enable access to high-quality, integrated metadata, including definitions, models, data flows, and other information critical to understanding data and the systems through which it is created, maintained, and accessed.

Data Quality Management: Per DMBOK, the planning and implementation of quality management techniques to measure, assess, and improve the fitness of data for use within an organization; Per DCAM, the goals, approaches, and plans of action that ensure data content is of sufficient quality to support defined business and strategic objectives of the organization.

Data Governance: Per DMBOK, provides direction and oversight for data management activities and functions by establishing a system of decision rights and responsibilities for data, generally in the form of policies, standards, guidelines, and assessment of progress on data management goals; Per DCAM, defines rules, and assures adherence to best practices.

DCAM2 Foundational Activities: Activities essential to justify, establish, and organize a data management program.

DCAM2 Execution Capabilities: Capabilities focused on the work specific to data management; similar to DMBOK's functional areas.

DCAM2 Collaboration Capability: Focuses on coordinating people, processes, and technologies to ensure that data management activities are integrated into the organization's processes and valued by the organization's culture, so that data assets are holistically managed. The Data Control Environment is the only capability at this time.

DCAM2 Application Capability: Analytics Management, the sole capability, focuses on data use: it's the place where an organization gets value from the data. All other components of the model contribute to this ability so that the organization gets value from its data.

Review Questions

1. A framework supports data management in the following ways:

   - Presents a model for understanding the big picture context for data management.
   - Provides a model of the relationships between component pieces.
   - Helps in planning the improvement of existing practices within an organization.

2. The DMBOK is aimed largely at practitioners (i.e., data management professionals). It summarizes the holistic goals and activities of data management, as well as the purpose, activities, and tools associated with each functional area.

3. The framework is presented as a wheel with functional areas as sectors of the wheel. Each functional area of the wheel is then defined by a Context Diagram that describes:
   - The goals of the functional area.
   - Inputs to processes executed within the functional area and who supplies these.
   - The activities of the area and who executes these.
   - Deliverables from the functional area and who uses these.

4. The DAMA Wheel summarizes DAMA's data management functional areas, but does not imply much about the relationship between these component pieces. It even raises questions: Are the areas represented in the Wheel intended to be sequential? Are all of them directly connected to Data Governance (the center or the wheel) in the same way? Where is data management itself?

5. DAMA introduced the "Evolved Wheel," which:
   - Distinguishes activities that are executed at different points in the data life cycle, and foundational activities that span the data life cycle.
   - Accounts for topics that are included in the DMBOK2 but are not defined as functional areas.
   - Positions Data Governance as an oversight function that influences all other aspects of data management.

6. DAMA's DMBOK has eleven functional areas, which are categorized as part of a life cycle phase or as foundational activity, thus connected to all phases of the life cycle. In this model, Data Governance serves as an oversight function for the set of activities and responsibilities. Each of these functions has a specific purpose and each influences the quality of data in different ways.

7. Identify how the functional areas of the DAMA DMBOK fit into the data life cycle as follows:

- Plan and Design Phase:
    - Data Architecture.
    - Data Modeling and Design.
- Enable and Maintain Phase
    - Data Storage and Operations.
    - Data Integration and Interoperability.
    - Document and Content Management.
    - Reference and Master Data Management.
    - Data Warehousing and Business Intelligence.
- Use and Enhance Phase is not a functional area of data management but the usage of data. It includes a wide range of activities that may identify data limitations or potential new uses of data in different ways. These discoveries may result in new instances of planning and design and other life cycle activities.
- Foundational Activities
    - Data Security.
    - Metadata Management.
    - Data Quality Management.
- Oversight Phase
    - Data Governance.

8. The DAMA functional areas influence the quality of an organization's data in the following ways:
    - Data Architecture provides the organization with multiple perspectives on its data, including planning for the standardization of data to facilitate integration and preparation for multiple uses.
    - Data Modeling and Design supports data consistency, standardization, and, through these, interoperability. Business rules can be discovered through data models so that they can be enforced, criteria for validity can be defined, and requirements related to data completeness.
    - Data Storage and Operations - the hard core, technical aspects of managing data - ensure that data is available and accessible, systems are performant, and that technical operations have been executed as required.
    - Data Security ensures privacy and confidentiality, prevents unauthorized access, and depends on having reliable, high-quality metadata in place.
    - Data Integration and Interoperability provides for the movement of data within and between systems so that data is executed consistently, reliably, fits well with related data, and has high integrity.
    - Document and Content Management ensures documents and unstructured data are organized in appropriate ways to allow for use and disposal, and depends on associating documents and other content with high-quality metadata.
    - Reference and Master Data Management enable consistent use across systems of the most accurate, timely, and relevant version of truth about essential business entities. Master Data allows interaction with customers and enables operational efficiency. Reference data provides the basis for measures of validity.
    - Data Warehousing prepares data for use, while Business Intelligence is one of the primary uses of data.

- Metadata Management provides definitions, models, data flows, and other information critical to understanding data and the systems through which it is created, maintained, and accessed.
- Data Quality Management provides the techniques to measure, assess, and improve the fitness of data for use within an organization, which is necessary for understanding expectations and achieving goals related to improved quality. Business rules and data standards are both forms of metadata, and both are necessary to define data quality requirements and to make them consistent and comprehensible throughout the enterprise.
- Data Governance provides oversight for all functional areas involved in data quality.

9. Data management components are categorized as foundation, execution, collaboration, or application, presented as a set of concentric circles to show how they are related to each other. The foundation circle is at the center of the model. Foundation is followed by the execution, collaboration, and application circles. Data management components are assigned to the circles as follows:
- Foundation
    o Data Strategy and Business Case.
    o Data Management Program and Funding.
- Execution
    o Business and Data Architecture.
    o Data and Technology Architecture.
    o Data Quality Management.
    o Data Governance.
- Collaboration
    o Data Control Environment.
- Application
    o Analytics Management.

10. The purposes of the foundation activities of the DCAM2 include:
- The data management strategy defines the rationale and goals of the program and how they will be achieved, providing a means to compare the current state to the target in order to show how organizational, functional, and technological gaps will be closed.
- The business case justifies the work in terms of costs and benefits and describes how the program will be measured and evaluated.
- The data management program is the formal organization established to ensure data management requirements are implemented, focusing on defining the key components of the data management program and how the program is structured in terms of people, process, and technology.
- The funding piece ensures that the program is sustainable.

11. Data quality improvement is often a driver for implementing better data management practices. The strategy and business case component provides a strategic perspective on data overall that raises awareness of connections between business functions and provides criteria for prioritizing data quality efforts. The program and funding component provides authority, accountability, and resources necessary to support data quality efforts.

12. The purposes of the execution capabilities of the DCAM2 model include:
- Business architecture takes a strategic approach to the design of business processes, so that they fit together and work efficiently.
- Data architecture defines the meaning and relationships between data.
- Technical architecture defines how technical infrastructure (platforms, applications, tools) supports the data architecture and enables the creation, storage, maintenance, access, and use of data.

- Data quality management is a set of processes intended to make data fit for purpose across the data supply chain.
- Data governance ensures that technical, business, and operational functions are accountable for the quality, maintenance, and use of data in the enterprise.

13. Business architecture is the basis for understanding what data business processes require as input, what data they produce as output, and what both sets of data represent in relation to the real world and to business concepts, such as products, customers, and coverages. Data architecture translates business knowledge into architecture artifacts at different levels of abstraction to understand the current state of data and propose a future state of data within the enterprise. Technology architecture plays a critical role in the creation, maintenance, storage, and use of data. Data quality management provides strategic alignment, clear definitions of dimensions of quality, clear processes and metrics, the ability to address root causes of issues and errors, and bi-directional communication between program team members and customers. Data governance contributes to both creating and enforcing standards and policies that help ensure data quality, as well as clarifying accountability for data.

14. Activities included in the Data Control Environment, the only capability of the DCAM2's collaboration circle includes:

- Defining and capturing data requirements.
- Ensuring data flows and processes are defined and understood so that data can be delivered to consumers.
- Ensuring resources and controls are in place as data moves throughout the organization.
- Ensuring control functions (e.g., Information Security, Data Privacy, and Change Management) are aligned and collaborate in sync with the Data Management program to ensure data is properly managed across all business functions.
- Identifying and reducing risks to and from data.

15. False. The control environment and execution components are constructs of the DCAM2 model, not the DMBOK.

16. The application of data to a business problem is the point where quality matters.

17. The DMBOK2 and DCAM/DCAM2 models differ in the following ways:

- The DMBOK2 is aimed at practitioners within the data management functional areas. DCAM is aimed at organizations looking to build their data control environment and measure their data management practices.
- The DMBOK Context Diagram identifies activities, functions, and deliverables, while DCAM does not describe how to execute specific functions. DCAM focuses on definitions, the importance of capabilities, and goals.
- DCAM brings together business, data, and technology architecture with less focus on specific roles and practices. DCAM2 does not focus on particular technical approaches to providing data for analytics and reporting. DMBOK2 includes chapters on data warehousing and business intelligence.
- DCAM2 addresses the need for leadership engagement and cultural change in its discussion of strategy and business case, emphasizing the need to justify the need for data management within the organization. DMBOK2 has specific chapters on organizational considerations and culture change.

18. The challenges or limitations of both DAMA and EDM frameworks include:
    - Different organizations have different ways of naming functions and the functional people who perform them (i.e., programmers, application developers, technical leads). Also, people on the teams contributing to the frameworks have different experiences. Together, these can complicate how to define data management within the organization.
    - Both DAMA and EDM present their frameworks as comprehensive data management frameworks. However, some people misunderstand the difference between data management and data governance, meshing the two together. This causes the team to lose sight of the idea that governance is oversight, while management is a more comprehensive category.
    - Frameworks do not solve problems. They should simplify understanding, enable learning, and support business strategy if implemented and applied by people who use them to solve problems.

19. The ISO model provides a comprehensive, high-level picture of the processes required to manage data quality linked to other processes within the organization. The model includes the familiar functions of data management (design/architecture, data movement, data operations, and data security management) but also includes data quality organization management, specifically human resources management.

20. The ISO model applies the Shewhart Cycle: Plan, Do, Check, Act, in the following ways:
    - ISO's view of "plan" aligns closely with the core capability of defining data quality standards, through documented expectations and rules.
    - ISO's definition of "do" aligns with data assessment, data quality monitoring, issue management, and data quality reporting.
    - For the ISO model, some aspects of "do" include an aspect of "check", e.g., monitoring data quality and managing issues.
    - For ISO, "act" is the improvement part of the improvement cycle: applying what is learned through the process.

21. False. Only the ISO model specifically links data management processes to Data Quality Organization Management and Human Resources Management.

22. When considering a framework, consider:
    - A framework is necessary to take a strategic approach to data management.
    - Choosing a framework that is best for our organization.
    - Apply what you learn from multiple frameworks without focusing on their differences.

23. False. The goal is to enable data management practices that allow the organization to get more value from its data.

24. The value in looking at different frameworks includes:
    - The organization can gain insights into both the current and future states by seeing how the frameworks organize assumptions about challenges.
    - The organization can see what is needed to improve capabilities over time by understanding the way different frameworks define the progression of steps needed to build capability.
    - By using consultants in the framework review process, organizations gain an outside perspective that can help define the problems needing to be solved.

25. The biggest risk is to see the framework as an end in itself. To minimize the risk, define the organization's requirements and identify the problems that need solving.

Data Quality Management Maturity

Educational Objectives

Upon completion of this assignment, you should be able to:

1. Explain what a Capability Maturity Model (CMM) is and how it can be used to understand and improve processes and the effectiveness of organizational capabilities, including data quality management.
2. Describe how CMMs may differ from each other based on the examples within data management (US Department of Labor; Data Management Maturity Model from ISACA-CMMI; the DCAM from the Enterprise Data Management Council).
3. Describe the limitations of capability maturity models and the risks associated with using one.
4. Explain the DCAM's approach to data quality management maturity and what we can learn from it.
5. Describe the ways in which using a CMM can contribute to process improvements within an organization.

For each assignment, define or describe each of the Key Terms and Concepts and answer each of the Review and Discussion Questions.

Key Terms and Concepts

Capability Maturity Model (CMM):

Data Management Maturity Assessment:

Critical Data Elements:

Review Questions

1. True or False: The CMM provides a standard against which to measure improvement but also an initial assessment of maturity.

2. List and define the levels of a generic CMM and describe the overall status of the capability.

3. List some of the questions that might be asked to identify the level of maturity of a component of a CMM.

4. How does an organization move from one stage to a higher-level stage in CMM?

5. A Capability Maturity Assessment helps document the current state of capabilities that an organization wants to improve. How does the output from such an assessment help the organization?

6. What are the benefits of a Capability Maturity Assessment?

7. How does a CMM provide value to an organization?

8. True or False: All organizations aspire to level 5 maturity.

9. What are the risks in using a CMM?

10. What are the benefits of applying CMM to data management?

11. Compare the four data management maturity models in the text in terms of levels of maturity.

12. Compare the four data management maturity models in the text in terms of components.

13. Identify the three capabilities and the ten sub-capabilities in the DCAM Data Quality Program Maturity Model.

14. According to the DCAM, what steps must an organization take to improve the quality of data?

15. True or False: A mature organization will have comprehensive data integrity controls on all data.

16. How can clear communications support the cultural focus in the DCAM?

17. In the DCAM, what purposes does an assessment of the current state of data quality serve?

18. Per the DCAM, what is the best way to handle errors? What are the benefits to such an approach?

19. True or False: The DCAM is not a traditional CMM since it focuses on establishing the foundation of an overall program rather than the evolution of capabilities over time.

20. How does a capability maturity model help an organization manage its data and serve its customers?

21. How does a CMM help with people, process, and technology?

Discussion Questions

NOTE: The questions below are intended to continue to challenge you to test your knowledge of the required reading by applying what you have studied to real-life situations.

No suggested answers are provided at the end of the assignment for these types of open discussion questions. Answers may vary by student and will depend on their organization's culture, resources, and processes.

Does your organization use a capability maturity model?

1. If so:

   - What was the process used to select or develop the model?
   - What level of maturity has your organization achieved?
   - What problems or challenges has the organization experienced?
   - What successes are attributable to the CMM?

2. If not:

   - Why do you think the organization hasn't adopted a CMM?
   - What challenges could prevent the adoption?
   - What early successes do you think could be achieved?

Answers to Assignment 10 Questions

NOTE: These answers are provided to give students a basic understanding of acceptable types of responses. They are often not the only valid answers and are not intended to provide an exhaustive response to the questions.

Key Terms and Concepts

Capability Maturity Model (CMM): A framework that enables an organization to develop, grow, and improve a capability over time by describing the movement of process components from their inception to a mature state.

Data Management Maturity Assessment: An application of the CMM concept to data management as an overall capability and to the components of data management.

Critical Data Elements: The organization's most important data per the DCAM.

Review Questions

1. True.

2. The levels of a generic CMM include:

   - **Level 1**: Initial/Ad Hoc: Little or no capability, some individuals practice elements of the capability.
   - **Level 2**: Repeatable: Emerging capability with some formal processes in place.
   - **Level 3**: Defined: The value of the capability is recognized and the capability begins to be an enabler.
   - **Level 4**: Managed: The capability is owned, articulated, and developed so that processes are executed consistently.
   - **Level 5**: Optimized: The organization measures itself against capability standards so that the process is highly predictable and reliable.

3. Questions that might be asked to identify the level of maturity of a component of a CMM include:

   - How is the process executed, with a focus on the level of standardization or automation through which the process is executed?
   - What controls are present (controls may be automated, policy-oriented, or both)?
   - How reliable and repeatable is the process? Can the process be executed consistently and deliver consistent results?

4. Each capability or sub-capability is rated along a scale that reflects maturity level. At each successive stage, process execution becomes more consistent, predictable, and reliable, taking on more characteristics of the next stage. In fact, the arc of improvement itself becomes more predictable. In order for an organization to move to the next stage, it needs

to meet the metrics for consistency, predictability, and reliability that are associated with that next stage.

5. The output from a Capability Maturity Assessment helps the organization:

   - Understand its starting point and identify strengths, weaknesses, and gaps.
   - Evaluate its level of maturity against the level required to meet business goals.
   - Benchmark against competitors or partners.
   - Plan capability improvements (e.g., efficiencies, training, automation).
   - Provide a baseline against which to measure improvement.

6. The benefits of a Capability Maturity Assessment include:

   - Provides a big picture/macro view of the capability and each component, along with details to back up that view.
   - Provides a defined pathway to move from the current state to the future state for each micro-element of the framework.

7. A CMM provides value to an organization in the following ways:

   - Recognizes that capabilities cannot be implemented all at once.
   - Recognizes that capabilities change over time.
   - Provides a communication tool to summarize current and future states.
   - Provides focus on meeting business goals.

8. False. Some organizations may only target enough improvement to meet business goals.

9. One issue is choosing an appropriate model. Capability Maturity Models differ in structure and level of detail. The organization must define the challenges and problems it needs to solve in order to select an appropriate model. A second risk involves a temptation to inflate assessment scores. Inflating initial scores to make the organization look better risks missing the chance to understand risks and gaps, thus priorities. Ongoing scoring needs to be accurate to identify how well risks are being managed and how well goals are being met.

10. The benefits of applying CMM to data management include:

    - Provides a method for ranking data management practices within the organization to characterize the current state and its impact on the organization.
    - Helps communicate to the wider organization that data management must be implemented in a phased manner.
    - Provides time for the organization to set goals, test them, and learn from the practices it is adopting.

11. The Data Management Maturity (DMM), the Gartner Model, and the US Department of Labor models have four levels of maturity, while the DCAM has six. The first level for DCAM and Gartner are similar, Not Initiated and Unaware, respectively. None of the models describes the levels in the same way, nor do they use the standard language of the original CMM.

12. DCAM has the most components, with eight, while the US Department of Labor's model has just five. The DCAM is the most detailed, while the Department of Labor's is the most abstract (people, technology, analytics, culture, and data). Gartner's model focuses on

components that could be used for any strategic initiative (vision, strategy, metrics, governance, roles/responsibilities, life cycle, infrastructure). DCAM and DMM specifically focus on data. Strategy is the first component in the DCAM and DMM but is the second component in the Gartner model. Strategy is not a component in the US Department of Labor model.

13. The three capabilities and their sub-capabilities in the DCAM Data Quality Program Maturity Model are:

- The Data Quality Program is established:
  - The data quality strategy and approach are defined and socialized.
  - Accountable parties have been identified and roles and responsibilities have been assigned.
  - The Data Quality roles and responsibilities have been communicated.
- The Current State of Data Quality is Assessed and Remediation Plans are Developed:
  - All relevant data have been identified and prioritized.
  - Data is profiled, analyzed, and graded.
  - Data remediation has been planned, prioritized, and actioned.
- Data Quality Program is Operational:
  - Data Quality control points are in place along the full spectrum of the data supply chain.
  - Data Quality Metrics are captured, reported, and used to drive data.
  - Root cause analysis is performed.
  - Data Quality Processes are audited.

14. According to the DCAM, an organization must take the following steps to improve the quality of data:

- Develop a data quality strategy that is implemented in stages, so that each stage moves progressively closer to alignment with business goals.
- Establish a plan for maintaining data integrity to be rolled out in phases, focusing on the data most critical to the organization.
- Create a shared cultural perspective on data quality, from executive head through operations, that grows over time as the organization adopts and hones its ability to get value from data quality management practices and communicates this value to business success.

15. False. Integrity controls will be established only on its most critical data.

16. Clear communications support the cultural focus in the DCAM by:

- Building consensus about requirements.
- Identifying common ways of measuring the quality of data (via agreed-upon dimensions of quality).
- Creating alignment with business goals related to risk management, analytics, customer service, and operational efficiency.
- Developing an assessment of the current state of data quality.

17. In the DCAM, an assessment of the current state of data quality:

- Determines the degree to which existing data is fit-for-purpose.
- Provides the basis for establishing business tolerance (thresholds) for different kinds of errors.
- Enables the organization to identify its most important data.

18. The best way to handle data errors is to prevent them in the first place by cleansing the data once at the point of capture based on verifiable documentation and business rules. The benefits include:

- Reduced correction along the data chain.
- Reduced need for validation.
- Enables data standard enforcement along the data chain.
- Less need for communication of data errors up and down the data chain.

19. True.

20. A CMM provides:

- A means to assess the existence of, adherence to, and effectiveness of practices and standards in individual functional areas.
- A basis for comparison of data quality practices used by related teams.
- A framework for prioritizing and addressing gaps and differences.
- A path forward in terms of people, processes, and technology.

21. The CMM helps identify:

- The data, knowledge, and skills that people in the organization will need to develop.
- The processes that need to be developed to support the organization's use of data.
- The technology required to manage data efficiently, reliably, and at scale.

Adopting Data Quality Management Practices

Educational Objectives

Upon completion of this assignment, you should be able to:

1. Identify the factors that should be considered when adopting data quality management practices within an organization and explain why they are important, especially for an insurance organization.
2. Describe the different ways data quality teams can be organized and how such teams are likely to evolve over time.
3. Describe the responsibilities and interactions of data quality teams at different levels of the organization.
4. Describe what factors can get in the way of the effort to create and sustain high-quality data, and how to mitigate these factors.

For each assignment, define or describe each of the Key Terms and Concepts and answer each of the Review and Discussion Questions.

Key Terms and Concepts

Organizational Culture:

Data Literacy Assessment:

Data Literacy:

General Literacy:

Centralized Data Quality Structure:

Replicated Data Quality Structure:

Federated Data Quality Structure:

Review Questions

1. Which of the following statements is true?

    A. Shareholders have no role in improving and sustaining data quality.
    B. Organizational culture includes how people embrace or avoid certain types of work.
    C. Organizational culture changes do not depend on people understanding how their role contributes to the organization's mission.
    D. All of the above are true.

2. What culture changes might be needed in an insurance company, given the ubiquitous nature of insurance data?

3. A data quality strategy should include:

4. True or False: The business strategy of insurance companies is very consistent from company to company.

5. What steps are needed to define a clear vision and mission for the strategic data quality effort?

6. Identify common insurance business strategies and the types of data that would be required for each?

7. True or False: The work of the data quality program to prioritize efforts and separate issues that have a material effect on business value is related to IT strategy.

8. Identify the important stakeholders and their impact on a DQ program.

9. Identify the knowledge and skills that comprise data literacy.

10. True or False: Data management programs should only include people with high levels of data literacy and experience to keep the focus on the challenges of data quality pain points and solutions.

11. True or False: Data pain points should be prioritized by the data quality team to ensure the most effective use of resources.

12. What process should be followed to address pain points?

13. Which of the following statements is true:

    A. The data quality team has sole responsibility for improving an organization's data.
    B. Businesspeople own the data created by processes but not the processes themselves, which belong to IT. As a result, they do not have to understand those processes.
    C. Although IT focuses on technological skills and lacks detailed knowledge of business data, they should have some knowledge of the enterprise, its goals, and the way data serves those goals.
    D. The most common approach to building a data quality structure is to start with a federated model and build towards a centralized model.

14. Identify some low-cost steps that businesspeople can take to improve data quality.

15. What steps can IT staff take to improve data quality?

16. How can organizational leadership change culture to reward a more effective relationship with data?

17. Identify the advantages of the different data quality structure models: centralized, replicated, and federated.

18. Identify the disadvantages of the different data quality structure models: centralized, replicated, and federated.

19. What value does having an enterprise data quality program team bring to knowledge and skill building?

20. How does the enterprise DQ team build an enterprise perspective on data?

21. How does the data quality team play a strategic role in growing capabilities?

22. Which statement is not true regarding the interaction of various teams?

    A. The enterprise program team works with business unit teams and business and technical stakeholders to ensure that they collaborate so that standards are developed and practices are adopted.
    B. The business unit level coordinates between the different system-level teams on business-level standards, practices, and data issues.
    C. The process level team works within the IT unit.
    D. All of the above are true.

23. What are the responsibilities at different levels of the organization for setting standards?

24. What are the responsibilities at different levels of the organization for assessing data quality?

25. What are the responsibilities at different levels of the organization for implementing controls?

26. What are the responsibilities at different levels of the organization for reporting on results?

27. What are the responsibilities at different levels of the organization for managing data issues?

28. What are the responsibilities at different levels of the organization for improving data quality?

29. Identify the obstacles to adopting data quality management practices.

30. Why is the lack of leadership support an obstacle to adopting data quality management practices?

31. Identify and describe the skills necessary for adopting data quality management practices.

32. True or False: Overcoming the inability to adopt new programs requires a sustained effort and leadership support to address cultural factors and to focus on the data quality.

33. Why is the lack of tooling and inability to scale such a risk for implementing a data quality program?

Discussion Questions

NOTE: The questions below are intended to continue to challenge you to test your knowledge of the required reading by applying what you have studied to real-life situations.

No suggested answers are provided at the end of the assignment for these types of open discussion questions. Answers may vary by student and will depend on their organization's culture, resources, and processes.

1. What factors were considered in developing the data quality organization in your company?

2. Describe the data quality structure in your organization.

3. How do different teams interact? Do their responsibilities mirror those described in the text?

4. How does your company address the cultural issues that can affect implementing a data quality program? Staffing? Structure? Training? Leadership?

Answers to Assignment 11 Questions

NOTE: These answers are provided to give students a basic understanding of acceptable types of responses. They are often not the only valid answers and are not intended to provide an exhaustive response to the questions.

Key Terms and Concepts

Organizational Culture: The way people work together.

Data Literacy Assessment: Focuses on the people in the organization, measuring their data knowledge, skills, and experience.

Data Literacy: The ability to read, understand, interpret, and learn from data in different contexts, including the ability to apply learning to new contexts and to communicate about data with other people.

General Literacy: The ability to read and understand written texts, as well as the ability to communicate in writing.

Centralized Data Quality Structure: One enterprise-wide organization that oversees activities for all business units and domains.

Replicated Data Quality Structure: The same data quality operating model, standards, and practices are adopted by each business unit, but there is no central organization.

Federated Data Quality Structure: An enterprise organization coordinates with multiple business units to adopt common practices and standards.

Review Questions

1. B.

2. Culture changes needed in an insurance company include:
   - Raised awareness of the ways data binds the organization together.
   - Bringing about a stewardship mindset, so that individuals feel increased accountability for the data they create or use.
   - Improved overall data literacy, so that people can communicate with each other about data challenges and so that they can collaborate to meet these challenges.

3. A data quality strategy should include:

   - An understanding of the organization's business strategy, the role of data in the business strategy, and the ways data enables and supports business activities and goals.
   - Engagement with stakeholders.
   - A data management capability maturity assessment.
   - A current state assessment of the data itself.

4. False. Insurance companies' business strategies will vary depending on their individual products and strategic goals.

5. The steps needed to define a clear vision and mission for the strategic data quality effort include:

- Prioritize the work to address findings of the current state assessment.
- Define an operating model for the program team to execute the work.
- Define roles and responsibilities for system, process, or business unit teams as part of the work.
- Define an implementation plan, including ongoing communications with stakeholders.

6. Common insurance business strategies and the types of data that would be required for each include:

   - Developing new products requires information on insurable risks, the feasibility of ensuring those risks, and how to price and market them.
   - Reaching new markets requires an understanding of the needs of these markets and the types of products likely to serve those needs.
   - Growing a customer base requires information on how to reach new customers.
   - Cross-selling to existing customers requires information on what they are likely to buy.
   - Underwriting and pricing products need information on risk.
   - Understanding changing risk characteristics needs information on external risks such as climate change, medical breakthroughs, laws, and regulations.

7. False. Business strategy connects the DQ program to business value, helping prioritize efforts and identifying important data.

8. The important stakeholders and their impact on a DQ program are:

   - Leaders need to understand how they each perceive the costs and benefits of data quality improvement and the costs of change itself.
   - The large number of internal and external users of data, each with its own culture and practices, needs to be accounted for in launching a data quality program to prevent unintended consequences.
   - IT, an important partner and stakeholder, needs to support changes in how data is collected, processed, moved within the organization, accessed, shared, and used as part of the data quality program.
   - Control functions such as compliance, risk management, and information security will be affected by the adoption of data quality practices.
   - Data governance and data quality management practices need to be very connected, reinforcing each other, especially with respect to standards, policies, and priorities.

9. Data literacy requires the following knowledge and skills:

   - General literacy, including comprehension, articulation, interpretation, and thinking skills.
   - Data organization.
   - Visualization.
   - Understanding and assessment of data quality.
   - Knowledge about data within the industry and the specific organization one works in.
   - Knowledge about the role of data within the organization and the connections in the different points of the product lifecycle.

10. False. People with different levels of knowledge offer different perspectives on the problems and different levels of understanding of the challenges involved, which are valuable and can lead to better solutions.

11. False. Stakeholders should prioritize the pain points to ensure they care about the assessment and outcomes.

12. To address pain points:

- Understand the problem from the stakeholder's perspective.
- Analyze the data itself to understand and quantify the problem, which may change the formulation of the problem.
- Identify the root causes.
- Do a cost/benefit analysis (CBA) to determine the best approach to remediation.
  - If the CBA indicates it is cost effective to remediate the issue, then implement the best option (ideally, the option that is cost effective and addresses the root causes of the issue).
  - If the costs of remediation outweigh the benefits, then communicate the decision that the issue will not be addressed and why it is not being addressed.
- Implement controls to prevent the problem from recurring. Unless cost-prohibitive, controls should be implemented even if the data itself will not be remediated.
- Measure, monitor, and report on the conditions of the data, informing data consumers about both the volume of problematic data and any changes in trend related to the data.

13. C.

14. Low-cost steps that businesspeople can take to improve data quality include:

- Clarify their data requirements (as both creators and customers of organizational data).
- Recognize that the data they produce is a product used by others in the organization.
- Act in ways that enable their data products to meet the quality requirements of data consumers (most of whom are their colleagues).
- When they think they see a problem, report it and ask follow-up questions.
- Influence and advocate for change that will result in sustainable improvements.
- Resist the temptation to implement workarounds.
- Be clear-headed about technology.
- Build their data skills and knowledge.
- Document and share their knowledge about data.
- Communicate knowledge and questions upstream and downstream.
- Building a strong partnership with IT.
- Build a strong partnership with the data quality and/or data governance program.
- Evaluate the priority and value of proposed process changes and data quality controls.

15. To improve data quality, IT can:

- Recognize that their real product is empowering the business to use data, not technology.
- Design and implement controls in applications to prevent data issues.
- Recognize that applications require basic data management controls, such as upfront edits, records in/records out, balance and reconciliation processes, even if businesspeople have not specifically asked for these.
- Ask businesspeople for data quality requirements instead of assuming that the data will always be okay or that no one has control over the data.
- Raise red flags when they see data problems or have questions about the data.
- Do not assume that businesspeople already have answers to questions that have not yet been asked.

- Provide a technological perspective on business process improvements.
- Help businesspeople ask better questions and see opportunities for better data through improved technical processes. Examples: data standardization, validation, edit/controls, master data.

16. To reward a more effective relationship with data, organizational leadership can:

- Clarify job descriptions to ensure people understand their responsibilities toward data and data quality.
- Incorporate data skills into job descriptions; provide training to improve these skills.
- Make clear that data is a product, not a by-product of business processes.
- Incentivize high-quality outcomes, including incentives to focus on the quality of data, rather than just the implementation of technology.
- Where appropriate, establish formal data stewardship at the business unit or process level (keeping in mind that all people who create or use data must be stewards of that data).
- Change IT funding models to account for requirements.
- Budget for remediation of data quality issues.

17. The advantages of the different data quality structure models include:

In a centralized structure, the program team can:
- Define and roll out a program relatively quickly.
- Define and test practices.
- Set data standards at the enterprise level.
- Facilitate the adoption of practices and standards.

In a replicated structure:
- Different business units can address different challenges as they see fit.
- Different business units can set their own priorities and serve the needs of their units.
- Different business units can take advantage of practices they have in place.
- Business unit staff are likely to have a deep knowledge of the business unit's data.

In a federated structure that takes advantage of both other models:
- An enterprise team can set standards at the enterprise level with the engagement of business unit teams.
- Business units retain some level of autonomy.
- All business units can learn from each other.

18. Identify the disadvantages of the different data quality structure models, including:

In a centralized structure:
- An enterprise team may be seen as imposing its requirements on business units.
- The scope of the data it is responsible for may be a source of contention.
- The team is unlikely to have deep knowledge of any business unit data.
- It will be necessary to have people who work closely with the data pay attention to it.

In a replicated structure:
- There are a few incentives to account for the enterprise holistically.
- There are a few incentives for different parts of the organization to interact or learn from each other.

- Success depends on how well units collaborate; the less collaboration, the slower the process of building data quality management capabilities will be.
- There is a likelihood of disparity between business units with respect to the adoption of data management practices.

In a federated structure:
- There may be contention about enterprise priorities, causing disparate levels of adoption.
- Because this model is implemented in a phased manner, there can be disparate skill and knowledge levels.

19. The enterprise DQ program team helps build out the skills and develop the knowledge necessary to define practices, templates, and tools. They also drive the adoption of the practices that establish, monitor, and sustain the production of high-quality data.

20. The team has the benefits of making changes or establishing standards so that the data from across the organization fits together. The enterprise DQ team will help develop standards at the enterprise level. If part of the enterprise data governance program, the team can bring their knowledge of organizational data to bear on the prioritization of governance activities. Team members in a business unit can gain an enterprise perspective by being exposed to upstream and downstream processes related to data from their business unit.

21. The program team guides the adoption of practices over time and helps to ensure consistent execution. As processes, goals, and technology change, the team ensures that new data requirements are defined and that systems and processes are designed to ensure data meets quality requirements.

22. C.

23. For setting standards, the responsibilities at different levels of the organization are:

- Enterprise Level
  - Set enterprise standards for data.
  - Define practices around setting data standards at other levels.
- Business Unit Level
  - Adopt enterprise standards where applicable.
  - Define business unit level standards where needed, following the practices set by the enterprise team.
  - Enable system and process teams to adopt standards.
  - Coordinate between data quality teams and the business unit.
- System Level
  - Limited responsibility for setting standards, and is directly responsible for implementing them.
- Process Level
  - Apply enterprise standards where possible.
  - Share requirements for standards with enterprise and business unit teams.

24. For assessing data quality, the responsibilities at different levels of the organization are:

- Enterprise Level
  - Develop methodologies for assessing data, including methods for quantifying issues.
  - Provide expertise and guidance on assessments.
  - May directly conduct the assessment when there is a defined set of enterprise data.

- Business Unit Level
  - o Assess prioritized business unit data based on standard practices.
  - o Identify issues and opportunities for improvement within the business unit.
  - o Identify likely impacts related to data used by other business units.
- System Level
  - o Assess the quality of data when they build and enhance the system to prevent risks related to incorrect assumptions about data.
  - o Work with the enterprise or business unit data quality teams to assess data quality when building or enhancing systems.
- Process Level
  - o Assess the quality of input and outputs from the process; ideally, following the methodology established by the enterprise data quality function.

25. For implementing controls, the responsibilities at different levels of the organization are:

- Enterprise Level
  - o Develop standard definitions of control types, including where and how they should be implemented.
  - o May directly implement controls when there is a defined set of enterprise data.
- Business Unit Level
  - o Oversee the implementation of controls in business unit systems and processes.
- System Level
  - o Development teams implement system, process, and data quality controls.
  - o Operational teams are responsible for monitoring operational functions, including data quality controls.
- Process Level
  - o Apply controls required for the process.
  - o Identify requirements for upstream controls.

26. For reporting on results, the responsibilities at different levels of the organization are:

- Enterprise Level
  - o Set standards for how to report on assessment results, monitoring controls, and data issues.
  - o Report on quality levels associated with a defined set of enterprise data.
  - o May aggregate data quality reporting across the enterprise.
- Business Unit Level
  - o Aggregate data quality reporting within the business unit.
  - o Prepare reports to be shared at the enterprise level.
- System Level
  - o Operational teams will report on system and data quality monitoring results, in partnership with the business unit data quality team.
- Process Level
  - o Report issues or risks with process inputs and workarounds required for process outputs.

27. For managing data issues, the responsibilities at different levels of the organization are:

- Enterprise Level
  - o Set standards for data issue management, including for quantification of data impact, business impact, and the costs and benefits of remediation options.
  - o Facilitate the resolution of issues that cross multiple business units.
- Business Unit Level

- o Prioritize business unit issues.
- o Facilitate interactions with business stakeholders to make decisions about how to address business unit data quality issues.
- System Level
  - o Operational teams manage issues related to the system, including initial analysis and quantification of impact.
  - o Alert system users, including downstream users, of the existence of data issues.
  - o Escalate issues to the business unit or enterprise data quality teams.
- Process Level
  - o Addressed through their assessment of data quality and reporting on results.

28. For improving data quality, the responsibilities at different levels of the organization are:

- Enterprise Level
  - o Facilitate the identification and definition of improvement opportunities.
  - o Coordinate on prioritization across the enterprise based on business, technical, and business unit data quality team input.
- Business Unit Level
  - o Facilitate the identification and definition of improvement opportunities across the business, based on business, technical, and enterprise data quality team input.
- System Level
  - o Share and help prioritize opportunities for improvement in partnership with enterprise and business unit teams.
- Process Level
  - o Identify opportunities to improve inputs or to automate the process to reduce risks related to outputs.

29. The obstacles to adopting data quality management practices include:

- Lack of leadership support.
- Lack of necessary skills.
- Organizational inability to adopt new processes.
- Lack of tooling or ability to scale.

30. Without leadership support, organizations do not change; people won't acknowledge that data quality is everyone's business and make the necessary adjustments.

31. The skills necessary for adopting data quality management practices are:

- Data analysis skills
  - o Understand data, the connections between data and business processes, and the risks related to data within an organization.
  - o Assess data, using different tools and techniques.
  - o Analytical and technical skills to do a deep dive analysis of data.
- Quality management knowledge
  - o Build and share knowledge of quality management techniques.
  - o Apply quality management methodology to data, from quantifying current state conditions to determining the root causes of data quality issues.
- People skills
  - o General communications skills applied to data, including the ability to summarize complex information about data and data issues, create effective data visualizations, and develop and share "data stories" for different audiences.

    o   Collaboration skills such as the ability to solve problems when working with people with different perspectives, different levels of knowledge/expertise, and different stakes in an outcome.

32. True.

33. While a lot of data quality work is "heads down, hands dirty", an enterprise program requires monitoring to be automated and ongoing. This requires tooling to handle the volume of data at the enterprise level.

Data Quality, Insurance, and Emerging Issues

Educational Objectives

Upon completion of this assignment, you should be able to:

1. Summarize a set of trends that multiple analysts agree are likely to strongly influence the future of insurance and connect these trends to the quality of data.
2. Explain what Generative AI is, why it has the potential to transform the insurance industry, and how it complicates questions related to data quality.
3. Describe how emerging regulation is attempting to mitigate the risks associated with GenAI and other forms of algorithmic decision-making, and why questions around the quality of data take on additional importance due to these risks.
4. Describe what data literacy is, why it is critical to the future success of the insurance industry, and why knowledge of data quality is a component of data literacy.

For each assignment, define or describe each of the Key Terms and Concepts and answer each of the Review and Discussion Questions.

Key Terms and Concepts

Protection Gap:

Digital Literacy:

Artificial Intelligence (AI):

Generative AI:

Large Language Models (LLMs):

Hallucinations:

External Consumer Data and Information Sources (ECDI):

Data Literacy:

Review Questions

1. List the common themes that will affect insurance in the future.

2. How is the insurance industry expected to transform in the future?

3. True or False: Filling the protection gap to reach underinsured populations requires innovation based on technology using existing data.

4. How can new technology be leveraged to support a customer-centric focus for insurers?

5. How has the recognition of the insurance industry's role as society's financial safety net resulted in some changes to the culture?

6. True or False: Insurers are recognizing the importance of the social responsibility to make purposeful, measurable environmental and social governance commitments. This process is progressing slowly due to technological constraints.

7. Why are trust and data quality included on the list of emerging trends in the insurance industry? What changes are needed?

8. How have new technologies and new kinds of data changed the way insurance organizations operate?

9. Which of the following data and technology innovations have had an impact on the insurance industry?

A. Social media and easy access to product information have changed insurance company operations.
B. There is a raised awareness of the risks associated with data that influences the ways individuals and organizations view data in terms of privacy, ownership, and individual rights and ethics.
C. The activities of bad actors who take advantage of increasing amounts of available data have resulted in government regulations managing risk and protecting individuals.
D. All of the above have had an impact on insurers.

10. Which of the following is NOT true regarding AI and Generative AI (GenAI)?

A. Many AI capabilities rely on predictable rules and are essentially advanced programming.
B. GenAI depends on technology that can process very large amounts of data, including structured data, images, documents, and other unstructured data.
C. GenAI content reflects the patterns in the inputs, resulting in a restructuring of the old information.
D. All of the above are false.

11. List common uses for GenAI.

12. What is the ethical risk associated with GenAI?

13. What is the explainability/validation risk associated with GenAI, and why is this such an issue for insurers?

14. What are the legal risks associated with AI?

15. What are practical obstacles to the adoption of some forms of AI?

16. High-quality, reliable data is necessary for the AI process. Which of the following statements is NOT true?

    A. It is difficult to describe the quality of unstructured data since it is more subjective to begin with.
    B. Unlike structured data, unstructured data incorporates the perspectives of the people who create it and is less subject to quality rules.
    C. Since unstructured data is not narrowed down to specific attributes of specific entities, it can include information about more things that can create noise.
    D. Unreliable structured data will likely result in unreliable AI results.

17. What value can GenAI bring to data management and data quality management?

18. Identify the guiding principles the NAIC issued related to the management of risk associated with the use of AI.

19. Which of the following is true regarding the Colorado regulation on the use of ECDI in insurance?

    A. The regulation applies to all lines of insurance: property, casualty, and life.
    B. The regulation restricts the use of EDIC, AI, algorithms, or predictive models.
    C. The primary focus of the regulation is to prevent racial discrimination
    D. All of the above are true.

20. What types of data are covered by the Colorado regulation of ECDI in life insurance?

21. According to the Colorado regulation, to use ECDI, AI, algorithms, or predictive models, what actions must insurers take?

22. What are the challenges related to ECDI data that the Colorado regulation addresses?

23. How does the Biden Administration's executive order on artificial intelligence differ from the Colorado regulation? What does it pertain to?

24. How does the California Consumer Privacy Act of 2018 and its 2020 amendment support privacy and control over one's personal data?

25. How do people develop data literacy?

26. What does it mean for an organization to be data literate?

27. Why is data quality a basic part of data literacy?

28. Why is it important for people in the insurance industry to be data literate?

Discussion Questions

NOTE: The questions below are intended to continue to challenge you to test your knowledge of the required reading by applying what you have studied to real-life situations.

No suggested answers are provided at the end of the assignment for these types of open discussion questions. Answers may vary by student and will depend on their organization's culture, resources, and processes.

1. What trends are you seeing influencing the future of the industry within your company?

2. Has your company begun to use GenAI? If not, how could GenAI be used effectively by your company?

3. How has emerging regulation affected your company? How might policies and procedures be changed to get ahead of some of the expected regulations?

4. How does your company address data literacy? What education is available? Who is encouraged to become data literate?

Answers to Assignment 12 Questions

NOTE: These answers are provided to give students a basic understanding of acceptable types of responses. They are often not the only valid answers and are not intended to provide an exhaustive response to the questions.

Key Terms and Concepts

Protection Gap: The difference between optimal insurance coverage and actual coverage.

Digital Literacy: Is the focus on navigating the digital environment, specifically, the ability to access, manage, understand, integrate, communicate, evaluate, and create information safely and appropriately through digital technologies for employment, decent jobs, and entrepreneurship.

Artificial Intelligence (AI): Refers to the capacity of computers to execute tasks that we associate with human behavior, especially tasks that make it appear that machines can think.

Generative AI: A form of artificial intelligence distinguished by its ability to create (i.e., generate) new content.

Large Language Models (LLMs): A type of AI that can recognize and analyze patterns and then present information back to users in the form of "natural language" (i.e., comprehensible sentences), or even images.

Hallucinations: Wrong answers generated by AI in which the AI engine has high confidence.

External Consumer Data and Information Sources (ECDI): A form of brokered data in which datasets are aggregated from multiple sources, cleansed, classified, and sold to organizations to supplement their own data and enhance their marketing, product development, and customer service functions.

Data Literacy: Includes a continuum of skills associated with collecting or creating data, applying it to answer questions, and sharing it with other people to solve problems.

Review Questions

1. Common themes that will affect insurance in the future include:

   - Transformation within the industry.
   - New markets.
   - Consumer-centricity.
   - Social benefits of insurance.
   - Social responsibility.
   - Trust and data quality.
   - External factors such as geopolitical instability, climate change, cybercrime, macro-economic factors, and other external factors.

2. The insurance industry is expected to transform in the following ways:

- The industry will be transformed by geopolitical instability, climate change, cybercrime, macroeconomic factors, and other external factors.
- As new risks emerge, insurers will need objective, reliable data to develop new products and underwrite effectively.
- Technological innovation, such as the increased availability and use of wearable devices to monitor health, drones to collect information, and sensors to evaluate driving characteristics, will transform how data is captured. Satellites, drones, and terrestrial sensors already provide data to support protection against droughts, earthquakes, and landslides. Advanced AI is being used to model and predict storm damage and assess damage after catastrophes.

3. False. While the technology is an important component, new data sources will be needed to supplement existing data to reach new markets.

4. Technology allows insurers to learn more about their customers in ways that enable them to present products optimally fitted to customers' needs, taking advantage of new technology to deliver products and services in the ways customers best receive them.

5. Recognizing this role of delivering social value is changing the dynamic of insurers' relationships with customers. The shift is away from a transactional approach to a broader, more holistic relationship-based interaction.

6. False. These efforts are data-intensive, but many organizations do not collect the type of data yet.

7. Insurer AI and analytics capabilities are only as good as the data sources supplying them. Insurers will need to make significant changes to meet the high-quality data requirements of AI and analytics to deliver value. They will need to eliminate silos and modernize data capabilities with an enterprise view. This will include enhanced master data management, integrating, managing, governing, and using both company data and large external unstructured datasets and third-party data.

8. New technologies and new kinds of data have changed the way insurance organizations operate in the following ways:

- Opened up opportunities to develop new products, customize them, and bring them to market quickly.
- Improved understanding of markets, customers, and cross-selling opportunities.
- Helped assess and retain effective partnerships and improve the performance of distribution channels.
- Improved models to more accurately assess risk and improve pricing and reserving practices.
- Improved the effectiveness of customer service practices and enabled self-service.
- Assessed the impact of adverse events in order to process claims as accurately and quickly as possible.
- Identified interventions to reduce the frequency and severity of adverse events, thus reducing claims.
- Detected claim fraud and reduced associated costs.
- Responded quickly and accurately to regulatory requirements.
- Improved the consistency and efficiency of reporting.

9. D.

10. C.

11. Common uses for GenAI are:

- Reduce the level of repetitive tasks required of employees, ideally freeing them up for more creative work.
- Improve customer service; for example, using input from past customer interactions to enable context-aware responses to new inquiries.
- Prevent fraud and enable risk management through pattern detection.
- Enable coding by translating descriptive requirements into draft code.
- Summarize information, such as meeting minutes or complex reports, to make them easier to comprehend.

12. GenAI creates content in a non-programmatic way, i.e., GenAI is a black box. It will not always produce the same results given the same input, and it is not clear exactly what is influencing the results. Biases inherent in the data can be reflected in the output, though they may not be visible on the surface.

13. Since GenAI is a black box, there is no way to validate whether its output is right or wrong. Since insurance is so heavily regulated, explainability is extremely important to meet regulatory scrutiny of risk assessment, rating, reserving, and claims handling.

14. The legal risks associated with AI are:

- If datasets used to train an AI model are owned by others, there may be a violation of intellectual property rights.
- The potential for acting illegally exists if the patterns the AI model learns include approaches that break the law.
- The risk of creating hallucinations.

15. Practical obstacles to the adoption of some forms of AI are:

- Governments are trying to get ahead of the GenAI curve with regulations to protect individuals from potential misuse of the technology. It isn't clear what effect these regulations will have on organizations to adopt and apply GenAI.
- In order to get value from the technology, the organization needs people with skills, such as knowledge of the tasks to be performed and the data used by the technology.
- GenAI is not good at analyzing data from legacy systems. In addition, reliable data, i.e., high-quality data, is needed for the technology to reach correct conclusions.

16. B.

17. GenAI brings value to data management and data quality management in the following ways:

- GenAI can be used to validate some content and identify its relevance to specific questions or problems.
- GenAI can be applied to detect problems in data through monitoring routines that rely on sophisticated pattern detection.
- GenAI may potentially be applied to reverse engineer code into natural language, which could be valuable for understanding data lineage and analyzing root causes of problems.

18. The NAIC-issued guiding principles related to the management of risk associated with the use of AI include:

- The necessity to respect laws.
- Pursue beneficial outcomes.
- Avoid harm.
- Ensure accountability, transparency, and security of data and systems that use AI.
- Act fairly and ethically.

19. C.

20. Types of data covered by the Colorado regulation of ECDI in life insurance include:

- Credit scores.
- Social media habits.
- Locations.
- Purchasing habits.
- Home ownership.
- Educational attainment.
- Licensures.
- Civil judgments.
- Occupation, other than those with a direct relationship to mortality, morbidity, or longevity risk.
- Consumer-generated Internet of Things data.
- Biometric data.
- Insurance risk scores derived by the insurer or third-party from the items listed above or similar data/information sources.

21. Insurers must establish a risk-based governance and risk management framework that facilitates and supports policies, procedures, systems, and controls designed to determine whether the use of such ECDI, algorithms, and predictive models potentially results in unfair discrimination with respect to race and remediate unfair discrimination, if detected.

22. Because their information is not collected from the application process, the applicant may not be aware that the data even exists. As a result, if the data is not correct, neither the applicant nor the insurer will know or have the opportunity to correct it. Furthermore, if this information is used as input to a model or algorithm with limited transparency, the algorithm may find patterns that people are not aware of that result in discrimination based on protected characteristics. If the data is incorrect, then the patterns from the algorithm may not be correct.

23. The Biden Administration's executive order is more wide-reaching than the Colorado regulation, applying to AI use in government, industry, and education. It advocates for America's leadership abroad. It references risks related to national security, biological materials, and perpetration of fraud, equity, and civil rights. It calls for standards to ensure the trustworthiness of data and algorithms and to protect privacy. The executive order also recognizes the potential value of AI in health care, education, government, and for consumers. It advocates for the use of AI to enable innovation and completion in business, while recognizing the need to support workers with fair labor practices.

24. The act not only restricts what data an organization can collect, but also how they store and share the data. The organization's data management functions must ensure they know how data moves

through the organization, where it is persisted, and by whom and for what purposes it is used. It empowers consumers to review the information an organization has on them, allowing them to request correction and also deletion of the information.

25. People need to learn about data itself and how it works. They need to have frequent opportunities to work with data, applying what they know and increasing their understanding and skills. Finally, they need to practice communicating data to others.

26. In order to be considered data literate, there needs to be a minimum level of data literacy throughout the organization. Also, people in specialized roles (data collection and processing, data management, reporting, business intelligence, and data science) need to have solid knowledge of the relationship between their role and the data they create and use.

27. Learning about data means people need to understand data quality. They need to understand the risks associated with data to reduce them. They need to understand that data can be created or collected incorrectly. Data can be stored, maintained, and shared in ways that break its integrity. It can grow stale and become outdated. Even if the data is sound, it can be misused or misinterpreted.

28. The industry is using different types of data from different sources for more types of analyses. To support this, the industry needs different skills, focus areas, and types of knowledge. The common foundation will be data literacy: knowledge of data-as-data, understanding how the data moves through the insurance life cycle, specific knowledge of the organization's data, and an understanding of the factors that can affect the quality of the data. This knowledge is fundamental to the organization's success.

www.ingramcontent.com/pod-product-compliance
Lightning Source LLC
Chambersburg PA
CBHW081926120726
47997CB00010B/3060